MINDFUL
LIVING WITH
ASPERGER'S
SYNDROME

EVERYDAY MINDFULNESS PRACTICES TO HELP YOU TUNE IN TO THE PRESENT MOMENT

CHRIS MITCHELL

Jessica Kingsley *Publishers*
London and Philadelphia

First published in 2014
by Jessica Kingsley Publishers
73 Collier Street
London N1 9BE, UK
and
400 Market Street, Suite 400
Philadelphia, PA 19106, USA

www.jkp.com

Copyright © Chris Mitchell 2014

Front cover image source: iStockphoto®

Library of Congress Cataloging in Publication Data
Mitchell, Chris, 1978-
   Mindful living with Asperger's syndrome : everyday mindfulness practices to help
you tune in to the
present moment / Chris Mitchell.
      pages cm
   Includes bibliographical references and index.
   ISBN 978-1-84905-434-8 (pbk. : alk. paper) -- ISBN 978-0-85700-867-1
(ebook) 1. Asperger's
syndrome. 2. Meditation--Therapeutic use. I. Title.
   RC553.A88M583 2014
   616.85'8832--dc23
                                          2013028699

British Library Cataloguing in Publication Data
A CIP catalogue record for this book is available from the British Library

ISBN 978 1 84905 434 8
eISBN 978 0 85700 867 1

Printed and bound by Bell and Bain Ltd, Glasgow

IN MEMORY OF
GENEVIEVE EDMONDS
1981–2008

In 2008, I was shocked to learn of the tragic death of Genevieve Edmonds, a fellow JKP author who had become a very good friend.

Tribute to Genevieve Edmonds made at Everest Base Camp in 2009 during a trek to raise funds for the National Autistic Society in her memory

Though Genevieve's life was tragically short, the difference she made to the lives of so many people and families affected by Asperger's syndrome, including my own, will continue to live on – as will the huge contribution she made to changing the way Asperger's syndrome is understood and perceived.

Through Solution-Focused Therapy, Genevieve had become a strong believer in focusing on solutions to living with Asperger's syndrome rather than problems, which is evident in approaches and therapies being applied to living and coping with Asperger's syndrome today. Without Genevieve's work, this book may not have been possible.

Genevieve continues to be missed by her family and friends, especially her mother Lynne, her father Alan and her sister Fiona, who in 2013 gave birth to a baby boy, Aidan Harald James.

Continue to rest in peace Genevieve, free from suffering.

CONTENTS

ACKNOWLEDGEMENTS

My family, including my parents, grandparents, siblings, aunts, uncles and cousins for all your continued support.

Gwennie Fraser, Mindfulness Teacher at Mindfulness in Life, who taught me during the eight-week mindfulness-based stress reduction course, for your calmness and understanding.

Peter Macdonald, Managing Director at Autism Works, for the confidence you have shown in me and the opportunities you have given me.

Lynne Moxon, Chartered Psychologist, for all your help over the years since my diagnosis.

Professor Tony Attwood, whose work initially helped me realise who I am as a person diagnosed with Asperger's syndrome.

Peter Harvey, retired Professor of Buddhist Studies, for all your help and guidance with meditation practice.

The Samatha Trust for your guidance during meditation retreats at the Samatha Centre, Powys, Wales.

Ajahn Munindo and the monastic community at Aruna Ratangari, Harnham, Northumberland, for your guidance during monastic stays.

Venerable Nandapala, Senior Abbot at Vivekarama Buddhist Temple, Sunderland, for your guidance.

And lastly, all individuals with Asperger's syndrome, and their families and carers, to whom I provided support. Working with you and knowing you has raised my own self-esteem, giving me so much joy to see that I have made a difference to your lives in a positive way.

INTRODUCTION
Mindfulness in a Secular Context

The concept of mindfulness has become so popular within psychology, psychotherapy, counselling and other related fields that there has emerged a number of varying definitions, some more accurate than others. Mindfulness is described in turn as a relaxation tool, a technique or a state of mind. Though mindfulness practice does have elements of each of these, for the purpose of this book mindfulness will refer to non-judgemental awareness within the moment, being here and now in the present and practising the art of observation while focusing on the breath.

Such contentiousness over what a particular concept is can be confusing for those new to it, and this is especially true for people diagnosed with Asperger's syndrome who may have difficulty accepting that there is no right or wrong answer or clear definition. As a person with Asperger's syndrome, I have learned to accept and appreciate that there often isn't a right answer when it comes to abstract concepts like mindfulness. However, it can still cause me confusion, which, as is the case for many people with Asperger's syndrome, can lead to anxiety. Ironically, one of the potential benefits that mindfulness practice can have for people with Asperger's syndrome is being able to cope better with anxiety.

Before going into more detail about the concept of mindfulness and its relationship with Asperger's syndrome,

I would like to start by placing it in a secular context in order to dispel some myths and misconceptions about it, particularly its connection to religion. It is true that mindfulness practice has its roots in religion and spirituality, particularly Buddhism and Hinduism. Other major faiths such as Christianity, Islam and Judaism also include some elements of meditation and mindfulness practice. Despite this, practising mindfulness doesn't have to be in a spiritual or religious context, and can be available to all, whatever one's perspective. Unfortunately, when mindfulness is first introduced people often think that it is a step towards conversion to Buddhism.

Due to their tendency to like structure, rules and routine, it sometimes happens that people with Asperger's syndrome begin to see mindfulness practice as a routine way of life in itself, often to the extent that it almost becomes a doctrine. If it is seen in this way, they may find that mindfulness practice has a negative effect, as they become anxious worrying about when or where to practise or that they haven't practised on a particular day. Another hindrance to mindfulness practice, and one that anyone who has little or no experience can encounter when taking it up, is the expectation that it will immediately and dramatically improve their quality of life. This can cause frustration when quick results are not seen.

Mindfulness practice in a secular setting and in the context of this book is *not* any of the following:

- conversion to Buddhism or Hinduism by the back door

- a cure or solution to all of one's problems and issues

- a doctrine or rigid routine-orientated way of life.

Initially, I found my way to mindfulness practice when exploring the principles and practices of Buddhism, feeling that I could relate to Buddhism as it was in line with my personal values and suited my Asperger's syndrome traits. I began to practise regularly and to explore the origin of the practice itself, which was developed by the Buddha from yoga techniques already in existence in India. My understanding and experience of practice methods began to unfold slowly. After experiencing monastic stays and meditation retreats, I found myself moving away from the original visualisation that I had of meditation, which was of a figure sitting cross-legged with the eyes closed. From the practices described in this book, you will find that meditation and mindfulness is much more varied than just sitting. It can include:

- standing

- walking

- stretching

- lying/reclining.

Like many people with Asperger's syndrome, I am very much a visual thinker and this means that I often need to have an image in order to understand a concept or process. However, I have slowly begun to understand that relying on such images can often mean that you do not see what is actually within or around the image. In the case of meditation practice, from just an image associated with it, you may see the religion or spiritual movement rather than the actual practice itself. After practising meditation for five years in a spiritual context, I undertook an eight-week mindfulness-based stress reduction course developed by mindfulness practitioner Jon Kabat-Zinn. I found that extending my practice and the perception I had of mindfulness beyond its spiritual dimension enabled me to bring qualities experienced during practice into normal life.

The eight-week course enhanced my mindfulness practice by bringing more variation into my practice, as well as contributing to more physical flexibility with stretching and mindful yoga exercises. I feel that the course helped to strengthen my understanding of mindfulness by opening me up to my life in the here and now, and helping me to understand how I am affected by Asperger's syndrome.

Opening up to Asperger's syndrome

It is well-documented that individuals diagnosed with Asperger's syndrome are affected by the condition differently. They can also perceive the Asperger's label very differently – some may feel uneasy about it while some may embrace it. Whatever the stage we are at in the diagnostic process – whether we are seeking a diagnosis, have just obtained a diagnosis or have had a diagnosis for some time – rather than hide from it or celebrate it, what if we open up to the diagnosis instead?

One of the main challenges of living with Asperger's syndrome is coping with ups and downs in moods, feelings and self-esteem. These ups and downs can be highly variable, as they can also be for people not on the autistic spectrum, and can range from joy and confidence to anxiety and depression. For people with Asperger's syndrome, though, perhaps because we often have obsessive-compulsive tendencies or difficulties with responding and adapting to change, it can be very difficult to manage these changes in emotion. This can be due to confusion over how to respond, coupled with difficulties in understanding the social circumstances that contribute to such feelings. There may also be the tendency to become stuck in such a mood because we cling on to or grasp it to the extent that the feeling controls us. Often, the immediate or instinctive reaction to ill feeling, both mental and physical, is to fight against it, to push it away or ignore it, but then we may find that the more we react in such a way, the more the feelings bite back and the more anxious we become.

When we feel trapped in such a phase, especially if in an unhappy or depressed state of mind, we start to become obsessed with thinking about our lives and this takes us out of the 'now'. In his pioneering work *The Power of Now*, Eckhart Tolle (2005) describes how our minds tend to wander into imagining futures that we may think are better than what we have here in the now, or perhaps into holding on to a time in our past which we felt was better or was when we were happier. Alternatively, the mind may have a tendency to find itself stuck in imagined futures or a remembered past worse than the present, and this only helps to escalate anxiety and depression. These thought patterns may revolve around worries about coping with situations that we are yet to experience, especially transitions, or unpleasant memories from the past such as the effects of bullying – something that many people with Asperger's syndrome have experienced. Tolle suggests that the way to start accessing the now is simply to notice when the mind is becoming trapped in such patterns of thought:

> The moment you realise you are not present, you *are* present. (Tolle 2005, p.45)

Rather than being constrained by feelings of stress, anxiety or doubt surrounding an Asperger's syndrome diagnosis, or being caught up in thinking of Asperger's syndrome as a hindrance, if you open up to who you are in relation to how your condition affects you socially and physically, you can gain a stronger understanding, awareness and acceptance of who you are in the present.

Note for professionals and practitioners

Though the aim of this book is to directly help people with Asperger's syndrome seeking mindfulness practice, the methods described can also be recommended by professionals, including psychologists, psychiatrists, counsellors, support workers and mindfulness practitioners. If you are a professional working with a person with Asperger's syndrome, before going ahead with any of the practices described in this book or, indeed, any other similar practice methods, do make sure that the client seeks the practice by personal choice, rather than feeling that it is being forced upon them. My own experience observing mindfulness workshops conducted in schools, including special schools, has shown that sometimes, if participants feel that the practice is being forced upon them, this only makes them feel more anxious when trying to relax or to be calm.

The individual nature of Asperger's syndrome can be quite a challenge for professionals and practitioners. Mindfulness practice is likely to have very different effects on different people with Asperger's syndrome and may work well for some but not for others. If the client is someone who understands instructions very literally or has a need for timetabled routines, this can affect how they take to mindfulness practice. It will help if you do not consider the practice descriptions in this book as being set in stone, or even as instructions, but as being guidance open to flexibility to suit different individual needs.

To apply flexibility to the practices described in this work, it may also help to explore other guided mindfulness practices, including practical demonstrations such as attending a class or watching a mindfulness/meditation DVD. In order to help your client get the best out of this book, and out of mindfulness practice generally, it may also help to remember that there isn't success or failure associated with mindfulness practice. Nobody is in a competition with either themselves or anybody else to achieve anything.

As a practitioner, using mindfulness practice with a client with Asperger's syndrome can be as fascinating a journey for yourself as for your client.

CHAPTER 1

ASPERGER COMFORT ZONES
Bringing Asperger's Syndrome
Out of Automatic Pilot

A major aspect of life that many people with Asperger's syndrome often have difficulty with is coping with or adapting to change. This can stem from a feeling of being constrained by their condition. They may be so in tune with the tendencies that their condition presents that they forget to tune in to their current, most immediate, experience. This is often referred to as 'automatic pilot' or 'autopilot' for short. People with Asperger's syndrome can find themselves particularly prone to going into a state of autopilot due to:

- a liking for routine

- a liking for structure, timetables (e.g. everything at the right time)

- a need for predictability.

Though it is helpful for many of us with Asperger's syndrome to have a set routine that suits our individual needs, we must be mindful not to create a comfort zone which is so comfortable that we lose touch with what lies beyond. Comfort zones created by routine and structure can take away awareness without us realising it. Often we only discover that we have lost this awareness by falling outside of our comfort zone. Rather like when walking along a flat, even path, the wandering mind is preoccupied with other thoughts, but then the path suddenly becomes uneven and we don't notice this until we actually slip or fall.

At the same time as structure and routine can create a comfort zone within which we feel safe, it can also become an obstacle, often relating to changes in circumstances beyond our control that may be difficult to anticipate.

When on autopilot, those of us with Asperger's syndrome can become so set in our ways that we lose touch with our surroundings and we may struggle to cope with:

- sudden or unpredictable demands (e.g. crisis response)

- unanticipated alterations to routine (e.g. sudden changes to timetable caused by unforeseen circumstances)

- change of structure/environment (e.g. moving office, moving house).

Though it may be good for many of us with Asperger's syndrome to have a routine that we are comfortable with, when this routine has to change out of circumstances, it can feel like the carpet is being dragged from under our feet.

When we live life on autopilot, taking the same routes to get to work or to go shopping because we feel comfortable with them, or completing daily routines out of habit, there is much that we become blind to. Usually, this is because our eyes see what we feel comfortable within, rather than what is beyond our comfort zone. Often, when we find ourselves set in such ways, we take the comfort zone for granted, to the extent that when a break occurs in our routine or a when a life pattern that has been normal for us changes suddenly, we may become very anxious. For the more rigid routine-orientated person with Asperger's syndrome, this can result in panic attacks.

It can take much effort for people with Asperger's syndrome, when they are set in a routine that they are comfortable with, to attempt to break this autopilot mode. From my own experience of Asperger's syndrome, I have often found it helpful to stick to a routine for my own personal comfort and to help me to cope with the high-level anxiety that sudden or unpredictable demands can bring. Though there have been times in my life, both before and after my diagnosis, where I have felt the need for and comfort within predictability, what I didn't realise until I first sought mindfulness practice was what I was also missing out on beyond the security of my routine.

The obsessive-compulsive tendencies present within many people with Asperger's syndrome mean that we can often take the notion of routine to the extreme and become almost robot-like without realising it. One of the main purposes of mindfulness practice is to experience coming out of our comfort zone. To enable this, as part of the practice, we assume different postures allowing us to notice different sensations that are often present without us realising it. The more we practise, the more we notice, thus becoming aware of what we may often miss when on autopilot in normal life.

There are many practical examples within my normal life pattern that I either miss or forget when on autopilot, in particular, actions or events that I don't experience very often. Such examples include:

- not noticing the traffic lights changing to green when driving

- missing appointments

- getting off the train at the wrong station.

Elsewhere, I have also found that being stuck on autopilot can lead to developing habits that are often not good, including:

- eating the same food for meals frequently

- wearing the same clothes frequently

- repeatedly tuning in to a television channel or radio frequency to watch or listen to a favourite programme, even though the series finished several weeks ago!

However comical these and other similar examples may sound, they can quite often have awkward consequences or lead to frustration for others! When taking the eight-week mindfulness-based stress reduction course, despite having practised meditation for quite some time, it started to become much clearer to me just how I often walk or drive somewhere without being aware of the journey; or when undertaking a task like writing an essay or giving a lecture or workshop, I am not always present, maybe because I am working within a system or formula. Sometimes, for people with Asperger's syndrome, it can be distressing when a system or formula is broken. Being able to adapt to and cope with such a change can be difficult.

Gradually becoming more aware of how I am, as I am, has enabled me to cope with changes in routine in a more positive way, rather than trying to block change through resistance. It has also helped me to notice how, often, the more we resist change, the more stressed and anxious we become. For the more 'routine-rigid' individual with Asperger's syndrome, the natural instinct may be to resist change and grasp at old routines. Development of mindfulness can enable us to develop greater control over such actions.

Comfort zones and acting on autopilot can also affect the thought processes of an individual with Asperger's syndrome and how that person presents socially. It is well-documented that people with Asperger's syndrome can be one-track-minded with narrow fixations. For some, when stepping beyond such fixations or special interests, it can almost be like stepping into another country where they are not familiar with the customs or language, particularly if they feel that they can't hold a conversation within a social environment without bringing it back to a special interest.

Another aspect of Asperger's syndrome that is also subject to autopilot is difficulty with flexibility of thought. Personally, I feel that the reason for this isn't so much because the Asperger mind is neurologically rigid, but it may also be that we slip into the comfort zone of our thought patterns. Many people with Asperger's syndrome can experience low self-esteem through feeling stuck within negative thought patterns, especially if their personal circumstances are difficult in a socio-emotional sense (e.g. social isolation). Our natural instinct is often to become overly preoccupied with such thought patterns, which may lead to depression and bring about more dangerous habits or behaviours, including self-harm, as a way of coping. Having experienced this personally, I am aware of how difficult it can be to break the cycle. Over time, though, I have found that by just being aware that one's thoughts are often not reality is reassuring, which mindfulness practice has helped me recognise with more clarity.

In order to switch off from autopilot and to stop being trapped in a comfort zone, it is often initially helpful to notice when we are withdrawing into certain thinking patterns, both positive and negative, or undertaking a particular action out of habit that may be triggered by Asperger or obsessive-compulsive tendencies. An advantage of mindfulness practice is that it can contribute towards breaking our cycle of routine, however rigid, through its variation in practice exercises involving different movements and postures. A challenge that those of us with Asperger's syndrome may experience is that we find it difficult to adapt to flexible approaches, including towards mindfulness practice itself.

Coping: Attempting practice during different times of the day in different places

Different mindfulness practices are described throughout this book. Before attempting any of the exercises, it will be helpful to find an approach which is appropriate for you. This will ensure that you experience the exercises and their effects to their fullest. When pursuing mindfulness practice, including meditation, mindful yoga, body scans and other stretching and breathing exercises, set a regular time and place for practice. If you are a beginner in mindfulness practice, this approach should be convenient to your needs as well as helping you initially establish regular practice. More routine-rigid people with Asperger's syndrome may initially find it difficult to motivate themselves to attempt mindfulness practice as it may feel like an obstacle to their routine. In which case, it helps to view practice not as an obstacle or hindrance, but as a way to step back from routine, even if it is initially for a few minutes, to just notice and get in touch with who you are, including your Asperger tendencies. During practice, whichever method you are using, it is helpful to:

- notice when you are doing something on autopilot, especially if undertaking a practice that involves physical movement (e.g. walking meditation, stretching exercise)

- notice any thoughts or triggers, perhaps related to your Asperger tendencies, allowing them to rise and pass, rather than becoming involved with or attached to them.

Although it is a good idea when starting out to have a set time and place to practise, you do have to be careful to avoid this becoming an inflexible habit. When this happens, the aim of the practice itself can almost work in reverse in that it can create routine within routine, becoming a difficult cycle to break in relation to Asperger tendencies.

Sometimes, when mindfulness practice becomes routine in itself, it can present limitations on the quality and effects of the experience and the ease with which it can be adapted into everyday life situations. At some stage, it may help to experiment with different methods of mindfulness practice at different times of day in order to bring variation into practice. With variation in practice it is helpful to:

- notice any differences in feelings, mental and physical, you may experience when undertaking practice at different times of day, perhaps when lighting or sounds are different

- notice any variations in sensations experienced when practising in different settings, including different sensations of, for example, sitting on different cushions/chairs or standing on different floors.

This may initially sound like trying to change or even cure what are perceived to be 'unhelpful Asperger tendencies', but the purpose of development of mindfulness, including mindful skills, doesn't mean that Asperger tendencies, traits and characteristics go away. Asperger-related characteristics are likely to still be present, because this is how an individual with Asperger's syndrome is in relation to how their condition affects them. But just by noticing how Asperger characteristics affect your thoughts can give you greater control over how they affect your subsequent behaviour or actions.

CHAPTER 2

CHANGEABILITY OF ASPERGER'S SYNDROME

Impermanence within Asperger Traits

One of the most fascinating and spectacular places in the world to watch changeability in action is the Perito Moreno Glacier in Patagonia, South America. Perito Moreno is one of the largest and most active glaciers outside Antarctica, calving approximately every 30 minutes. From an Asperger perspective, as well as the scientific theories as to why the glacier calves, what intrigued me most when I observed this natural phenomenon was how I felt it related to the feeling of impermanence regarding how being diagnosed with Asperger's syndrome affects me.

Asperger's syndrome is often described as a lifelong condition. This is true in that it is present throughout one's life and, whatever one's opinion on the issue, it can't be cured. However, we have to be careful not to confuse the notion of lifelong with permanence, in terms of how Asperger's syndrome affects those diagnosed with the condition, or how they cope with its effects.

When seeing an image of a glacier, the natural assumption may be to think that it is a still, permanent sheet of frozen ice, frozen to the point that it doesn't move, when in actual fact it is constantly moving and changing very slowly. Similarly, a person with Asperger's syndrome, while uncomfortable with or resistant to change, is nevertheless changing constantly mentally and physically in relation to their diagnosis, often without realising it. Eventually, the pressure from the glacial flow causes the glacier to calve when one least expects it, making a thunderous sound when a piece of ice falls off. Similarly, a person with Asperger's syndrome may respond to pressure triggered by mental and physical change within themselves with a breakdown or panic attack.

What makes it difficult for many people with Asperger's syndrome, including myself, to notice and acknowledge changeability of the way they are affected by their condition is largely due to their idiosyncrasies – the way they think (e.g. rigid thoughts) or behave (e.g. repetitive movements) or how they respond to different or unanticipated situations outside their comfort zone. As a person with Asperger's syndrome, I have found that the way I think is often dominated by:

- obsessions

- habits, including traits and quirks

- memories

- fantasies

- thought processes.

Though such thought patterns are consistent with the way the mind works, just being able to notice and observe where we slip into such thinking patterns can take some effort. Mindfulness practice can help us to cope when we find ourselves stuck in habitual thinking because it can enable us to step back from the flow of life to observe changes that occur within the body. The actions of many people with Asperger's syndrome often originate from triggers within the Asperger mind that perhaps relate to an obsession or interest, often when we are least aware. Simply by noticing that we are reacting to a particular situation, as well as noticing the trigger for the action, is often helpful.

Such triggers of thoughts and actions within people with Asperger's syndrome can also originate from feelings and sensations experienced within the body, including tension or physical discomfort in relation to posture as well as sensory issues including sound, touch, taste and smell. Though such feelings and sensations are constantly present, noticing how they affect our behaviour helps us to step back from the flow. Stepping back from the flow, into unfamiliar surroundings that are away from our normal routine, gives us a chance to notice more clearly our habits, traits, characteristics and thought processes, including their effects. When watching a glacier calve, we see a familiar and almost-regular process occur where a chunk of ice breaks off from the glacier and falls into the lake or sea. Though it is a similar process each time that a calving occurs, what we may not pay attention to is that each calving action is unique. Each chunk of ice that breaks off is a different size and shape, each sound it makes is different and each impact that it makes when it hits the lake or sea is different. Similarly, in normal life when on autopilot, there are actions that occur within the body and mind, most notably the breath, a neutral recurring process, breathing in and out constantly. Though it is a similar process each time we breathe in and out, what is not often apparent to us is that each breath in itself is different in length and in the effects it may have on sensations felt throughout the body.

Being able to notice the uniqueness of each breath during mindfulness practice was a starting point for me in coping with difficulties I had experienced in adapting to change. By giving the breath attention, we notice the effect it has on sensations and feelings throughout the body, such as tension. It can also help us to notice and understand the origins of:

- thoughts

- impulses

- obsessions.

These factors can become triggers for actions or reactions to processes such as change, both mental and physical. It is natural that we may act on our Asperger tendencies, including those listed above.

Though we may be happy with the way we are with our Asperger traits, especially if they enable a special interest or skill, where difficulty may lie is in being able to notice that such traits are not necessarily permanent, and are subject to change.

As well as coping with Asperger traits being subject to continual change and renewal, a person with Asperger's syndrome, especially at the point of diagnosis, may also worry that such traits may affect them throughout life, including aspects of life that they are yet to experience. Many people with Asperger's syndrome may also be in denial of their condition, feeling that if they disclose it they might miss out on certain aspects of life, including friendships, intimate relationships, starting a family, achieving qualifications or having a successful career.

At the point of my diagnosis, though it was a relief after the depression and social isolation that I was experiencing, at the same time I was troubled by thoughts of how it would affect me in future years. Would I always be obsessive in my thoughts and behaviour and would interpersonal relationships always be difficult for me? The notion of the condition being lifelong made me feel that there wasn't anything that would stop me from behaving in an obsessive way, from feeling over-anxious or worrying excessively. However, the more I began to adapt to the diagnosis, the more I began to appreciate my

Asperger characteristics in a positive way. Although I still experienced anxiety relating to what my immediate and long-term future would mean for me, how I would be understood, and, pertaining to the lifelong theme, how I would never change, the different way of understanding myself that I have developed through mindfulness practice enabled me to notice my Asperger traits. Just through being able to notice them, I am able to observe how they affect me in relation to my surroundings, socially and physically.

By starting to notice within mindfulness practice how different feelings and sensations are subject to change, I have also opened up to how the effects of Asperger's syndrome can be subject to change. Much anxiety I have experienced has often originated from not being able to notice changeability. The act of paying attention to changeability has given me a stronger awareness that changes can occur in the way that my Asperger's syndrome affects me, and overall has provided relief to me in knowing that change can happen at all.

I have found that just being aware of the possibilities of changeability within Asperger's syndrome can help to reduce stress. Then, noticing reduction in stress enables me to bring clarity and attention to changeability as it occurs in the present moment. Where I have struggled to cope with change, and where many people with Asperger's syndrome I have met have also struggled, is in being able to settle into a new school, college, university or job. Such changes involve being in a new environment around people that we are not familiar with. There may also be many new skills to learn and different social conventions to adapt to. What was most difficult for me, though, was unlearning methods and conventions that I was used to in previous environments. But just through noticing with mindfulness ever-occurring variations occurring within the body, particularly around the breath, I have been able to apply this to my life beyond practice. I have found that I am able to notice when I find myself stuck in practices or social conventions that aren't appropriate within a new environment.

Such awareness helps me to be able to work with change as it occurs in the present. Whereas before, as soon as I was aware of change, whether occurring or coming, I would have a tendency to hold on to what I had. Being able to be open to and adapt to change can be an opportunity for personal growth and development, including enabling independence.

Coping: Noticing variation during sitting practice

How we feel within our posture can affect our state of mind during practice. As we are all different in body shape and have different degrees of physical flexibility, there is no standard posture that can suit all. Finding and assuming a comfortable posture for the practice can sometimes take a little patience.

Step 1: Sitting mindfulness practice can be done sitting on a chair or on the floor. If sitting on a chair, use one that is upright with a firm though not necessarily hard surface (e.g. a dinner table chair), rather than one in which you may sit back or slump (e.g. a couch). During practice, sit on the edge of the chair away from the back, as this allows your back to be positioned straight, opening up the breathing channels. If sitting on the floor, you may choose to sit kneeling or, if flexible enough, you may sit cross-legged. If kneeling, use a cushion to lift the backside from the floor allowing your knees to be close to the ground with the thighs sloping. The next stage of developing an appropriate posture involves keeping the back straight. A helpful technique can be to pretend that there is a piece of string attached to your head that is gently keeping you upright, while allowing your shoulders to drop and relax.

Step 2: Start by finding a posture that is comfortable and allows you to keep your back straight. Once comfortable in posture, start by placing your hands on your lap, right hand on top of left hand with the palms facing upwards (or the other way round if you are left-handed) with the thumbs lightly touching, and then gently close your eyes. Start the practice by focusing on the breath, paying attention to each breath coming in and going out. Once your attention is in tune with the breath, start by noticing the difference in each breath in terms of its length and weight, noticing just how unique each breath is.

Step 3: While maintaining your focus on the breath, slowly start to expand attention throughout the body, noticing sensations, including how you are influenced by the breath or your posture, also noticing any areas of discomfort. Your natural tendency may be to resist, but, rather, try to imagine the breath travelling there. Notice also variations in sensations, how they are changing constantly, and how they influence thoughts, including those related to Asperger-related obsessions or fixations.

Step 4: As a person with Asperger's syndrome, your natural tendency may be to withdraw into such fixations, obsessions, thoughts and opinions. Each time you find this happening, gently bring your attention back to the breath. All minds, both those of people with Asperger's syndrome and those not on the autistic spectrum, will wander every so often. Just simply noticing this is helpful.

The purpose of this practice is not to 'eliminate' your Asperger tendencies, but rather just simply to notice them, including noticing how they may change every so often. Simply being aware of change as it unfolds within can be helpful in noticing and being with change as it occurs beyond practice, especially if you may otherwise feel resistant to change. The more you notice your Asperger tendencies by expanding noticing beyond practice, the more you may gradually find that you have more choice over acting on them, rather than being constrained by them. This will allow greater flexibility, including being able to adapt your Asperger traits as strengths to different situations as they unfold.

CHAPTER 3

ASPERGER'S SYNDROME IN THE PRESENT MOMENT

Tuning the Effects of Asperger's Syndrome to the Present

When I have been on meditation retreat at the Samatha Centre in Powys, Wales, one of the most special aspects of the practice, partially relating to my childhood fascination with astronomy, is practising under the stars. Since it is located in rural Wales away from the excesses of light pollution, more stars are visible on a clear night. While one of the purposes of the practice is to tune in to the present, the stars are, however, many light years away. They are reminding us that our past is with us here and now in the present. Rather than hold on to our past, or simply dismiss it, the purpose of mindfulness practice is to tune both our past and future to the present. This chapter explores how the effects of Asperger's syndrome can take us out of the present and looks at techniques to help tune Asperger's syndrome, its past and future, to the present.

People diagnosed with Asperger's syndrome are often described as being very good at worrying, particularly regarding coping with and meeting unpredictable demands or when awaiting outcomes of decisions or results, including a diagnosis or assessment itself. Though I can relate to this, being diagnosed with Asperger's syndrome, an aspect of worrying that took me a long time to realise was just how much tendencies to worry can lead to us losing touch with the present moment.

In everyday life, there are many controlling factors to Asperger's syndrome. Obsessions, preferences, likes and dislikes, from the very mild to obsessive-compulsive tendencies, can result in us losing touch with the quality of the present moment. Sometimes, the implications of being diagnosed with Asperger's syndrome itself can bring us out of the present moment. As well as a clinical diagnosis, Asperger's syndrome can represent an individual's past, present and future through:

- relief

- regret

- doubt.

For myself, and for many other people with Asperger's syndrome, the initial feeling at the point of diagnosis is often one of relief or joy, especially if diagnosed late in life. In this sense immediately in the present, we have a reason for why we are the way we are or why our life has been as it has. At the same time, at the point of diagnosis, we may feel regret for what we have perhaps missed out on, especially if the diagnosis explains much about our past. But what is often a source of anxiety at the point of diagnosis is worry as to how it will affect our future, including in situations which we are yet to experience.

As discussed in Chapter 2, the effects of Asperger's syndrome are not necessarily fixed or permanent, despite the condition being lifelong. Sometimes, when it is first diagnosed, we can easily see Asperger's syndrome as a hindrance when looking at its negative aspects. For instance, you might feel that you will miss out on being able to do adult things such as get a job or a partner or lead a normal independent life. Immediately, this can take you out of the present in that you worry about what you feel you can't have in your future, forgetting what you have in the present. This can also lead to low self-esteem.

Low self-esteem and anxiety can also mean that a person with Asperger's syndrome may miss out on developing life skills in the present. Stages of our life where the effects of Asperger's syndrome can become apparent include living away from parental control and influence for the first time (e.g. going to university), where we have to learn skills often needed to live an independent life, including social skills (e.g. negotiating skills); and in employment, where we have to learn social skills required in obtaining a job, as well as learning the practical skills to do the job. Low self-esteem together with high-level anxiety through worrying about whether or not we can cope with such changes can interfere with the levels of attention, patience, effort and concentration often needed in the present when learning new skills. Table 3.1 lists some feelings that a person with Asperger's syndrome may experience on a daily basis and what they can lead to.

Table 3.1 Some feelings experienced by those with Asperger's syndrome and what they can lead to

Feelings that can be present in day-to-day life	Such feelings can lead to
Confusion	Obsessiveness
Worry	Anxiety
Uncertainty	Tension
Fear	Low self-esteem

These feelings and what they can lead to can take a person with Asperger's syndrome out of the present moment, particularly if they become lost within them. The more anxious you find yourself about your future, the more you can forget what you have in the present. This can lead to distractions or procrastinations over tasks in hand or non-awareness of current matters, including personal or health-related issues.

Stress and anxiety can also stem from our own thoughts about what we want ourselves to be, as well as believing our thoughts and opinions to be facts. This leads to frustration through not measuring up to unrealistically high standards or expectations that we set ourselves. Anxiety can arise from frustration over not being what we would ideally like to be. Such thoughts about what we may aspire to be tend to arise from what we may perceive to be acceptable or successful, which can stand in the way of us being happy within ourselves in the present, and being able to accept who we are as we are in the present.

Just as for people not on the autistic spectrum, for those with Asperger's syndrome the past and future, to variable degrees, are with them in the present. Due to the effects that the condition can have through strong memory and recall, it can often be easy to remember the past and we can become attached to it, affecting us in the present. In the opposite direction, a person with Asperger's syndrome who finds unpredictability difficult to cope with can become attached to thinking about and planning their future, both immediate and long-term. Though it is often necessary for us to think a little about our immediate future, for a person with Asperger's syndrome it may sometimes not be apparent how certain circumstances might mean they have to alter any plans they have. Uncertainty that this can bring can lead to high-level anxiety, which can mean that they may miss out in the present.

As a person with Asperger's syndrome, I have found mindfulness practice helpful in opening me up to the richness that can be experienced in the present, as well as to the possibilities that the present moment can have. With mindfulness, I have found that I am able to pay attention to how it is in the present. Previously I would try to avoid facing up to situations that would otherwise have been difficult, which would often be a source of further stress and anxiety. I find the following exercise helpful for this purpose.

Coping: Three-minute breathing space

This is a simple exercise that is possible at just about any time of day. Its purpose is to enable you to step back from the flow for a short time, enabling you to return feeling more 'refreshed', and thus more in tune with the present. Despite the title, the exercise doesn't have to last exactly three minutes – it can be slightly shorter or longer, depending on your commitments, time constraints and how much time you may feel that you need to experience the effects of the exercise.

Step 1: Before starting the exercise, you need to find a posture with a straight back, without slumping or straining, in which you are comfortable. As the main subject of focus during this exercise is the breath, the back needs to be kept straight throughout the exercise where possible so that the breathing channels are open, allowing the sensations of the breath coming in and out to be felt. The exercise can be done standing or sitting, either on a chair or on the floor. If sitting on a chair, make sure that you are sitting on the edge of the chair with your back upright and that you are not leaning against anything.

Step 2: Once you have found a comfortable posture you can begin the practice. Start by simply focusing on the breath coming in and going out during the first minute. On the in-breath, notice the sensations of the breath coming in through the nostrils, going down the breathing channels, through the lungs and down to the diaphragm. Notice the chest expanding and the lungs rising. Then on the out-breath, notice the chest contracting and the lungs falling as air is expelled, noticing also the sensations of the breath going out through the nostrils.

Step 3: During the practice you may find that your mind wanders. An Asperger tendency may be to worry or possibly to doubt the purpose of the exercise. If you find that your mind wanders or you start having any feelings of doubt, don't worry, as this is what minds do. Remember that one of the purposes of this exercise is to reduce excessive worrying! If you find yourself worrying about issues from the past, about the future, or any issues you may have in the present, just bring your attention back to the breath, a neutral process which acts as an anchor for this practice.

Step 4: While focusing on the breath, you may start to notice your thoughts, including those relating to any issues you have that are a source of worry. Our natural tendency when thoughts arise may be to become lost within positive thoughts, perhaps relating to an Asperger-related special interest, or to resist or push away negative thoughts. When this occurs, acknowledge the thought, and each time just gently bring your attention back to the breath and its sensations. In this way, the breath becomes a tool for you to detach from thoughts and worries before they lead to anxiety.

Step 5: In your own time, once you feel that your attention is established on the breath, start to notice sensations in the soles of the feet on the ground, before gradually working your way up to the instep, and around the heel and the ankles. Working your way up the body, now start noticing sensations in the calves and shins before working your way up to the knees and the thighs, and then around the backside and the waist. Now focus on the area around the diaphragm, which can often be a source of feelings of tension. Wherever you feel any tension, just acknowledge it. If you feel that you are becoming attached to a feeling of tension, just bring your awareness back to the breath, imagining the breath travelling there.

Step 6: Now start to slowly expand awareness around the body using the breath, gradually work your way up to the chest area and the lower back, before moving on to the upper body, around the heart, the upper back and around the shoulders. Again, if you feel any pain or any discomfort, just imagine the breath travelling there. Now focus on the arms, around the elbows and the forearms, the hands and the fingers. If at any moment you feel uncomfortable, adjust your posture slightly, making the adjustment part of the practice, each time bringing attention back to the breath. Now transfer awareness to the neck, moving up to the back of the head, the scalp, the forehead and the face, around the mouth and nose and the chin and cheeks.

Step 7: Once you have scanned through the body, at ease with its sensations, acknowledging any feelings of tension, expand your awareness to the body as a whole, almost as if the whole body can breathe, accepting who you are, as you are. Using the breath, begin to expand your awareness to the space you occupy, including personal space. Personal space is not often easy for people with Asperger's syndrome to recognise the need for, but opening up to this stage of the practice can bring awareness of this.

With practice, the effects of this exercise, including awareness, can gradually be brought into everyday life. Try bringing any different awareness levels you feel you have experienced during the practice into the next moments of your day.

Chapter 4

MINDFUL MOVEMENT
Acknowledging Physical Capabilities and Limitations through Simple Stretching

It is well-documented that motor co-ordination when playing sports is a problem for many young people with Asperger's syndrome. As a person with Asperger's syndrome myself, I have found that activities which involve motor co-ordination can be helpful in physically adapting to your surroundings, including changing body postures. Mindful yoga is particularly useful as a means to get in touch with yourself physically.

There are said to be over 80,000 known movements within yoga. Obviously, it is not possible to go through them all in a day. The advantage that this has, though, is that it presents a choice of movements or postures that suit the physical make-up of the body. Part of your practice will be finding out which movements you are able to perform comfortably and which you find difficult. This enables you to make an effective assessment of your physical capabilities and become aware of any physical limitations, thus developing an acceptance of who you are as you are.

As it isn't possible to practise so many different movements on a regular basis due to physical limitations or time constraints, this allows for revisiting different movements every so often. Many yoga movements, particularly those that involve lying down on the floor or stretching the legs and arms, are often unusual movements for us beyond practice. Yoga practice helps us become more in tune with our physical nature to the extent that we notice in normal life when we are doing things out of habit or routine.

I have found that taking up unusual physical positions through the variation of movement within yoga practice helps me to cope with change much better. There are many aspects of life, including acceptance of change, that years ago I would have found uncomfortable. Yoga and other forms of mindfulness practice have gradually awakened me to the notion that the physical body in which we live is subject to physical change, and that as the body changes physically, how I see and interpret surroundings through the body affects me mentally. Just noticing and appreciating such ever-occurring changes within the body gives me relief knowing that biological and mental change occurs, rather than resisting it through being stuck within habits.

Often, when we put our body into postures that are not normal for us, this helps us to cope with and adapt to bodily change and can also help us to get in touch with and experience bodily sensations that we may otherwise take for granted. Such sensations, particularly increased due to sensory issues or motor skills difficulties that Asperger's syndrome may present, can include:

- discomfort
- unpleasantness
- pain.

When on autopilot outside of practice, our natural tendencies are to react by either pushing these sensations away or maybe just trying our best to ignore them by not thinking about them through:

- fear

- irritation

- annoyance.

Not only do the above responses distract us from the way things actually are with the body as it is in the present, but they can also have a reaction towards the way it is in that the more that they are repelled, the more they can keep coming back. This only adds to stress. Mindfulness practice, including mindful yoga, encourages a different approach towards such feelings, though it can take a bit of effort and patience in order to experience the full effects. Work with whatever sensations are present during a stretching exercise, rather than reacting to them or trying to push them away. However, if the sensations become too painful or unbearable, rather than immediately ceasing the practice, it helps to slowly move away from the stretch. Our natural tendency is to react by ceasing the stretch immediately, but this may only cause further injury (e.g. pulled muscles).

Remembering that all individuals on the autistic spectrum are different in terms of physical capabilities as well as levels of coping, including with bodily sensations, sometimes the feelings can be those of:

- comfort

- pleasantness.

However happy one may feel when sensations are like this, it can be very easy to become lost within such feeling to the extent that one doesn't want to let go of them through:

- attachment

- being set in routine.

What the above reactions are doing, though, is denying acceptance of how it is right now in this moment. However difficult or painful a particular movement or posture may be to take up, there is quality of feeling within if we make the effort to investigate and work with it rather than resist. In relation to difficulties that we may have in being able to understand the feelings and emotions of others, experiencing discomfort is helpful in understanding difficulties others experience, thus enabling development of compassion.

Another aspect of Asperger's syndrome that the practices described in this chapter can help is in coping with sensory issues. When we notice different sensations within the parts of the body that are involved in the movement, through using the breath, it helps to also focus on effects that the movement has on parts of the body not involved, and to notice any differences. The breath is a useful tool for enabling this. Through focusing the breath on areas of discomfort and where we feel comfortable in a part of the body not involved in the movement, it can help us to fully acknowledge and cope with different sensations.

Practice can also make it possible to gain a greater understanding of both our physical capabilities and limitations. What makes mindful yoga advantageous to the needs of many people with Asperger's syndrome is that it can be practised in solitude, in our own space; and, most importantly, it helps us to get in touch with ourselves physically while not being in competition with anybody else or with ourselves. In this way, you are able to get in touch with your physical make-up, including within areas of the body often taken for granted. Just through getting in touch with areas of the body that are not involved or affected by certain mental states can help you detach from any feelings of low self-esteem or high anxiety. This enables you to observe and acknowledge them rather than be controlled by them.

Though one of the purposes of yoga/stretching exercises, and mindfulness practice generally, is to be present with sensations, another purpose is for us to acknowledge physical limits, so we should not be encouraged to take up postures or attempt stretches that lead to unbearable pain. If pain becomes present, it is your body letting you know its limits.

Coping: Simple stretching exercise

For this exercise, it is helpful to practise at a time and in a place where you can be by yourself and are unlikely to be disturbed. Naturally, when attempting a stretching exercise for the first time, or when returning to such an exercise after a long break, you may feel a little clumsy and may also experience physical strain. Difficulties in motor skills that your condition may present might also be an initial hindrance to attempting mindful yoga and stretching exercises. Levels of coping with and responses to physical strain vary dramatically between different individuals on the autistic spectrum, relating to several factors including individual physical make-up and sensory processing. If you do have any persistent physical problems with your back, neck or arms it may be necessary for you to consult a doctor or physician before doing exercises involving stretching.

Step 1: Start by standing up straight with both feet slightly apart rooted to the ground, with the arms relaxed at the side. Relax the neck and the shoulders, keeping the head upright, still and straight.

Step 2: Start by simply noticing the breath, noticing the sensations of each breath coming in and going out. Now start noticing any sensations you can feel during the breath, including perhaps the diaphragm lowering and the chest expanding outwards on the in-breath, and the diaphragm rising and the chest contracting inwards on the out-breath.

Step 3: When you feel ready for the first movement in the exercise, start on an in-breath by slowly lifting your arms above your head. When your arms are directly above your head, you may want to link the thumbs, while stretching the arms as high as is physically and comfortably possible without excessive strain. Hold this position for just a few seconds and notice the effects and sensations of the stretch down both sides of the body while maintaining awareness of the breath.

Step 4: Then on an out-breath, un-link the thumbs and let the arms slowly start to come down, maintaining awareness of each stage of the movement until the arms are again by the sides. Rather than seeing this as a 'break' in the exercise, tune in to the sensations of the after-effects of the stretch, noticing any feelings of relief. If you find that you are becoming attached to or comfortable within such relief, just bring your attention back to the breath.

Step 5: In your own time, when ready, on an out-breath, start by slowly lifting the right arm above your head, keeping the arm straight, as if you are reaching out to hold on to a branch or railing that is just out of reach while stretching as far as is comfortable for you. Keep in mind that you are not in competition to see how far you can stretch. You may notice that the heels come off the ground. Using the breath, tune in to the effects of the stretch down the right side of the body, from the arm down to the hip. In relation to Asperger tendencies, if you feel any discomfort in this posture, your natural reaction may be to resist it through straining. If at any time you feel that you want to break out of the posture, rather than bringing the arm down, try bringing attention back to the breath. While maintaining awareness of the sensations of the stretch, tune in to the sensations of the left side of the body, noticing any differences in sensations of the side not involved in the movement.

Step 6: On an in-breath, when ready, start to slowly let the right arm come down again while remaining stretched out straight, again being aware of each stage of the movement. When the arm is back down by the side, using the breath, tune in to the after-effects of the stretch. This time, though, notice any differences in sensations on each side of the body, possibly noticing how after-effects of the stretch on the right side affect the left side not involved in the stretch.

Step 7: After you have experienced this stretch, repeat the exercise with the left arm. Again, maintain awareness on the breath and on each stage of the movement, from lifting the arm up to reaching out, heels coming up off the ground, to the arm coming down again, while noticing the effects of the stretch down the side of the body and the difference in sensations on each side of the body. Try also this time to notice where any effects of the stretch counteract with the side of the body not involved in the stretch, helping you to understand the body as it is, interconnected. This enables an acceptance of who you are, as you are, in terms of physical make-up, capabilities and limitations in relation to how you are affected by Asperger's syndrome regarding motor co-ordination.

Through regular practice of this exercise, you may notice that your stretching abilities and limitations, including how long you can sustain different stretches and postures, vary greatly. Outside practice, where possible, also be present with any effects that you may have experienced from doing this exercise, perhaps from how your posture is when doing physical exercise (e.g. running) or even the position of your back when sitting at a computer during working hours or when studying.

If and when you experience any difficult periods within life outside of practice, particularly if you feel that things are not going right with any plans or ambitions you may have, you may find that yoga and stretching exercises are particularly effective in enabling you to cope and persist by facing up to difficulties rather than hiding from them. If you can maintain such persistence and openness, you will notice the value of being present with your life as you are and as it unfolds, rather than being what any thoughts, fantasies or ambitions dictate to you that you are.

CHAPTER 5

GETTING IN TOUCH WITH EMOTIONS

How to Be Mindful of Your Emotions and Become Flexible towards the Emotions of Others

People with Asperger's syndrome are still sometimes stereotyped as having no emotions, or can come across as being emotionally blind to the thoughts and feelings of others. As I have found from personal experience and from the many other people with Asperger's syndrome I have met and their families, that people with Asperger's syndrome do often experience very deep emotional thought. When viewing glaciers, one of the most intriguing aspects to the eye is how blue they appear in colour. This is because blue is the only colour on the spectrum that the ice doesn't absorb. Similarly, in many people with Asperger's syndrome, their emotions are often absorbed by their condition. This chapter looks at techniques for getting in touch with our emotions, enabling us to understand how our emotions work in relation to Asperger's syndrome as well as how to relate our emotions externally.

As expressed earlier in this book, how Asperger's syndrome affects us is subject to change. Such changes in turn affect how we understand and interpret our surroundings, including how we perceive them emotionally. Often when responding to change, particularly during difficult periods, a whole new set of emotions are needed to manage such a change. This may be very difficult for a person with Asperger's syndrome. Coming to terms with being diagnosed with Asperger's syndrome itself often requires a whole different set of emotions to open up to the diagnosis. Other such times that often require such a new set of emotions include:

- adolescence
- developing an intimate relationship
- coping with a serious personal illness
- caring for a relative or friend diagnosed with a serious or terminal illness
- coping with a major loss.

An aspect of being diagnosed with Asperger's syndrome and its relationship with emotional development that I have found throughout my life is that you spend much time learning social conventions when trying to make sense of the social world. This enables you to access and interact with the social world where needed, but it can also mean that there is little scope to learn about the heart. As a result, many people with Asperger's syndrome, especially during adolescence, can feel socially underdeveloped, often leading to isolation and depression. During such periods a person with Asperger's syndrome, especially if they feel that they are emotionally misunderstood or can't express their emotions, may be vulnerable to acting on their emotions.

As well as developing an understanding of how the body is interconnected, including how bodily sensations affect the body as a whole, development of mindfulness can also enable us to understand how the body and mind, including our emotions, are interconnected. To understand this, it helps to start by investigating why we have emotions. Reasons suggested by Orsillo and Roemer (2011) for why we have emotions include:

- to communicate to us our needs

- to help prepare us for action, including during difficult times

- to enhance our life experiences

- to develop and deepen connections with others around us.

Our emotional needs are often communicated in sensory ways, usually through feelings of physical heaviness or fatigue. Being able to recognise this as a person with Asperger's syndrome can be difficult. As well as finding it hard to read the body language of others, reading our own body language when it is communicating our needs can also be difficult. Asperger tendencies, including worry and anxiety, as well as obsessiveness and sometimes sensory issues, can also trigger emotional reactions to the extent that a person with Asperger's syndrome can be acting on their emotions when they are least aware of it.

For some adults with Asperger's syndrome, unhappy experiences from their past can be a source of emotional unhappiness. Such experiences can include:

- bullying, including emotional and physical

- difference of opinion

- heated conflict, both verbal and physical.

Sometimes, for people with Asperger's syndrome the effort to detach from, rather than dwell on, bad memories is almost equivalent to soldiers coming to terms with the effects of shell-shock. Added to this, aggravations and disappointments (e.g. being unsuccessful at numerous job interviews, difficulties with social and intimate relationships) that people with Asperger's syndrome may experience in the present can also be a source of negative thought. Developing mindfulness using some of the techniques described in this book, especially those that focus largely on the breath, can enable you to suspend negative thoughts that you may otherwise become attached to. Just through applying attention, observing our thoughts and thinking about their source, and using the breath as an anchor, we can develop a non-judgemental approach towards the way we are in relation to others, rather than holding on to negative thoughts we may have towards others, which only escalate negative relations that can lead to conflict.

With development of mindfulness, you can gradually develop an ability to listen to your emotions. The body scan exercise described in the previous chapter, enabling you to recognise sensations, is helpful in this. Being able to first notice and acknowledge your emotions and what triggers emotional responses, including Asperger characteristics, can enable you to open up to these emotions. Quite often, if we try to dismiss our emotions, they bounce back and almost dictate our actions. Opening up to emotions, to a point where we can almost negotiate with them, can enable us to respond appropriately. Having more control over our emotions allows us to put into context how our actions may affect others.

The tunnel-vision tendency that many people with Asperger's syndrome can have may naturally make it very difficult to recognise or understand potential consequences of their actions. Being able to detach from our emotions can make a huge difference in enabling this, which also helps in making connections with others. Through opening up to our emotional and physical difficulties, feelings of social isolation and misunderstanding or occasional experience of physical pain and discomfort can enable us to relate to difficulties that others experience. This also makes possible the development of compassion – sympathy, concern and understanding of the difficulties or misfortunes of others – while being able to detach from our own issues.

Since my Asperger's syndrome diagnosis, I have occasionally experienced low self-esteem. I have found, though, that with mindfulness I am able to listen to my emotions much more clearly and open up to them rather than trying to push away deep emotional thought. I also feel that being able to listen to my emotions has opened me up to how my emotional thought can affect other people around me, thus giving me a stronger understanding of the emotions of others. The following exercise may help you develop understanding and compassion that can be extended to others around you, including family, colleagues, social circles and others in general.

Coping: Loving-kindness practice

The purpose of this practice is for you to develop an understanding of your emotions, including how they relate to others. It can also enable you to open up to the humanity of Asperger's syndrome. Instead of looking at how you may be different from others in relation to your Asperger's syndrome, the practice encourages you to find where your condition perhaps has similarities with others. This can help open you up to feeling and expressing sympathy as well as developing compassion.

Step 1: This practice can be done standing or sitting, on the floor or on a chair. Make sure that your back is upright. If you are sitting on a chair, make sure that your back isn't leaning against the back of it. Once you have found a posture in which you are comfortable, you can begin the practice by gently closing your eyes and focusing attention on the breath, coming in and going out.

Step 2: When you feel that your attention is established on the breath, you can now begin the practice by expanding your awareness to the heart area, cultivating feelings of loving-kindness towards yourself:

> May I be well and happy, may I be at ease and live in safety.

You will later extend this feeling to others during the practice. See what emotions arise. Emotions could be:

- positive
- negative
- neutral.

Step 3: When emotions arise, notice any tendency that you may have to put labels on them. When you feel that you have cultivated loving-kindness towards yourself, now you can start to slowly expand it, starting with the room in which you are practising. Now extend feelings to the property where the room in which you are practising is located. Then gradually expand this to the street or estate in which you live and then to the town or city in which you are and the surrounding region, gradually extending your circle wider. A good way to do this may be to visualise a rough sea gradually calming to the point that it becomes still, calm and concentrated.

Step 4: Slowly expand the feelings that you have cultivated towards yourself to everyone to your left, and everyone to your right, everyone in front of you, everyone above you and everyone behind you. Within this, include feelings of goodwill to all those with Asperger's syndrome. Think about how you want them to be well and happy, to be at ease and live in safety.

Step 5: Gradually begin to extend these feelings to all people not on the autistic spectrum. Using these feelings, overcome factors that divide people with Asperger's syndrome, including yourself, from people not on the autistic spectrum by looking at what we share. You could perhaps start with the notion that we all breathe the same air as well as share the same planet.

Step 6: Now start to focus on any similarities that you may have with people not on the autistic spectrum, including common interests or any similarities you may feel you have in outlook on life here and now in the present. Such an outlook could include wanting to be well and happy, at ease and live in safety. You want this for everyone around you, regardless of labels or categories.

Step 7: When you feel ready, finish the practice and see if you can bring any positive feelings you have gained from the practice to the rest of your day as each moment unfolds, as well as extend them to those close to you and beyond.

Within practice and away from practice, also notice where your Asperger tendencies, perhaps including personal preferences and differences of opinion with others, can absorb these feelings of kindness. Then notice instances where they are with us, but where we perhaps don't always apply them. In relation to difficult experiences we have had with others, either in the past or in the present, it helps to remember that we can't control what others put out towards us, but we can control what we put out to them. If others can't express kindness towards us, rather than dislike them, it helps to feel some compassion for them. Applying compassion helps because they are perhaps likely to suffer a lot through not being able to express kindness, rather like how you can feel that you miss out on various life experiences because of how you are affected by Asperger's syndrome (e.g. with social skills).

By applying compassion together with awareness and by being able to understand why another person has directed such verbal action towards you, you can gain control over your actions and how you respond.

CHAPTER 6

RECOGNISING BODY LANGUAGE
Releasing Tension and Understanding the Body within the Body

Body language and non-verbal communication are an aspect of life that many people with Asperger's syndrome often struggle with. Asperger's syndrome can almost be like 'social dyslexia' in the sense that people with this syndrome see non-verbal signals but interpret them differently, as a person with dyslexia sees words and letters but interprets them differently. As well as having difficulty reading the body language and non-verbal cues of others, people with Asperger's syndrome may also experience difficulty in being aware of their own body language, including how it can appear to others around them. This chapter looks at the benefits that mindfulness practice can have in enabling people with Asperger's syndrome to release tension and recognise body language.

The Buddha taught us to see 'the body within the body' (Ajahn Chah 2007). We can do this by becoming aware of different sensations through the body that are consistently present within us but we don't often notice, how these sensations are interconnected throughout the body, and how they can affect how we come across on the outside. Such feelings throughout the body can include:

- tightness
- heaviness
- numbness.

Often, people with Asperger's syndrome are described as being blind to or unable to express non-verbal communication and social cues, including facial expressions and eye contact. In reality, though, we are capable of developing these skills. But quite often we find that we have to learn such skills from observation, whereas to people not on the autistic spectrum, such skills are often developed through intuition. As a person with Asperger's syndrome, the biggest challenge that I have often found with non-verbal communication is being aware of how my own facial expression and body language present.

Like many people with Asperger's syndrome, I have found myself in situations where I have been misread by people around me due to the way my body language, facial expression or eye-contact comes across. When this occurs, it can be a confusing and sometimes intimidating experience, especially if the person reacts in an aggressive or threatening way. Such examples can include:

- prolonged eye-contact (staring)

- absent eye-contact (suggesting not paying attention)

- slumped posture (suggesting boredom)

- repetitive movements of hands and feet (suggesting seeking attention).

Throughout the body, there are many different sensations that are present, only a few of which we are aware of most of the time. We interpret many of them through what we see with our eyes. This often leaves little room to focus on the many other sensations that are constantly present with us, arising and fading, and how they affect the body as a whole, including posture and facial expression. Being able to notice how such feelings and sensations affect us is difficult for anyone in normal life, not just people with Asperger's syndrome. The even greater difficulty for a person with Asperger's syndrome to overcome, though, is being able to notice how sensations from within reflect on the outside, whether positive or negative.

Jon Kabat-Zinn (2004) reminds us that we are not just a resident of our head. In relation to the way being diagnosed with Asperger's syndrome affects me, I find that much of my thinking and thought-processing is largely visual. Like other people with Asperger's syndrome I have met, I often feel I need a visual image to explain or demonstrate what is occurring, including its context. Though such a way of processing information can have its advantages, from mindfulness practice I have gradually begun to notice how tired the region around the eyes can become. Different mindfulness exercises are done with the eyes closed or open, with some involving them being both open and closed. When the eyes are closed during practice, it can give us the chance to tune in to sensations and feelings throughout the body that don't involve the eyes, including the breath. This helps to focus on how the breath itself affects the body as a whole from the soles of the feet right up to the top of the scalp, including facial expression and posture.

When sitting, standing or lying in a posture that isn't normal for our body to assume, we may notice some feelings of physical discomfort. Often our natural tendency is to resist. When we resist, it can have an almost domino-like effect on our body movements, including our facial expression and posture. What is often helpful during practice is to open to it rather than resist. It is a difficult technique to master for many, and can be particularly difficult for a person on the autistic spectrum who experiences sensory difficulties. To enable this, it initially helps to focus the breath onto the area of the body where the discomfort is occurring and imagine the breath reaching the discomfort itself.

Certain areas of the body, particularly around the stomach area, can become tension reservoirs, where feelings of nervousness and anxiety build up. Though it can often be apparent when such sensations occur that we feel nervous or anxious, what is not often as apparent is how such sensations may then begin to affect the body as a whole, including how we present on the outside. In this way, how we may feel within can radiate beyond, ultimately having effects on others around us, which can be positive or negative depending on how we may feel within.

Where the effects of Asperger's syndrome can come into play with feelings and sensations throughout the body is often in relation to the obsessive-compulsive tendencies that people with the condition can have. They may find that they are controlled by or attached to them. Within me, I find this occurs through becoming attached to feelings of tension that stem from stress, anxiety and nervousness. This usually originates from worrying about coping with unpredictable demands or experiencing situations that I feel are outside of my comfort zone. Usually, I find that when tension builds up in areas or reservoirs within the body, often around the waist, it begins to spread throughout the body, influencing the neurons. This affects social presentation and actions. Often in my life I have found not being able to control such tension a problem, as it affects the way I am towards my surroundings, including towards people. This also includes how my non-verbal presentation can affect others, when I least know it.

At one time, my natural reaction to tension would have been either to resist it by ignoring it through trying to push it away, or become controlled by it to the extent that

I would withdraw into it through my Asperger tendencies. Through mindfulness practice, though, I have found that being able to cope with such issues often starts by acknowledging my feelings, simply by just being aware of them. This includes noticing how particular feelings influence thoughts, and how thoughts subsequently influence actions. Quite often, to become aware of how we appear beyond ourselves it helps us to come home to our body and observe what occurs internally, whether comfortable or uncomfortable.

On the outside, I have found that observation of non-verbal social gestures has contributed to me learning such skills to be able to interact with the social world. Internally, though, a technique that I have gradually found helpful in enabling me to become more aware of my own body language is through mindful observation of sensations throughout the body during mindfulness practice. This includes when practising exercises which involve stretching and those practised while sitting, standing or lying still. The exercise that I find most helpful for this purpose is the body scan, which is often practised while lying down.

Coping: Body scan

This is a simple guided body scan that can be practised in a time frame of between ten and thirty minutes, or longer. How long you would like to practise the exercise for is up to you. It may depend on other commitments that you have, or maybe your physical capabilities – especially if you find lying on your back for a lengthy period of time uncomfortable! One of the purposes of this exercise is for you to gain an understanding of the body as it is, including its physical capabilities as well as its limitations. The main purpose, though, is to come home to your body, to gain an acceptance of who you are, as you are.

Step 1: To do this practice, find a time and place where you can be by yourself and where you are unlikely to be disturbed. Be sure to wear clothes that you feel comfortable in. Start the practice by lying down on your back with legs and arms spread and the palms facing upwards. You can do this practice on a rug, a mat or any surface on which you feel comfortable. If cold, you may also want to put a blanket over you.

Step 2: Once settled into the lying down posture, start by giving the breath attention for a few minutes. Breathe slowly, at breath lengths that are comfortable for you, while feeling the diaphragm moving inwards and outwards. If you feel the mind wandering or you feel you become lost in thoughts or worries, just bring attention back to the breath, allowing any thoughts relating to memories, fantasies or planning to arise and pass.

Step 3: Start the actual scan by focusing attention on the toes of the left foot, and imagine the breath travelling there. Then gradually work your way up to the sole of the foot, the instep and around the ankle, before moving up to the shin and calf and then up to the knee and thigh. Each time, imagine the breath reaching these areas, giving them your attention, as if they could breathe themselves. Next, repeat this process starting from the toes of the right foot.

Step 4: While focusing on these particular parts of the body, continue to notice and feel the breath coming in and out. Remember throughout the practice that you are not trying to achieve anything, and that you are not in competition with yourself or anyone else.

Step 5: Gradually begin to notice sensations around the backside and lower back, including its contact with the floor, before focusing around the waist area. This may often be a reservoir for feelings of tension. If you feel any tension or physical discomfort, perhaps notice how it may spread through the body, to the extent that it influences thoughts and feelings, negative and positive. If you find that you are becoming lost in or attached to any thoughts or feelings, just gently bring your attention back to the breath.

Step 6: Next, gradually start to move up from the waist to the stomach area and the upper back, before continuing gradually to around the upper body and the shoulders and then into the arms, then the forearms, before coming down to the hands and fingers. Each time imagine the breath travelling there, almost as if these areas of the body themselves could breathe. Such areas of the body experience sensations, but we often take them for granted.

Step 7: The next stage is to transfer the focus of your attention to the neck, before working up to the back of the head, around the scalp and around the forehead, again each time imagining the breath travelling there. Now focus on the face, around the eyes and nose, perhaps tired from sensory processing, and then around the mouth, cheeks and chin.

Step 8: At this point, your attention will have covered just about the whole body. Now imagine if the whole body itself could breathe, noticing any effects that each breath has on the body as a whole, including on posture and facial expression. Notice also any feelings or sensations that play a part in how your posture and facial expression form. In the last stages of the practice, remember that you are not trying to achieve anything, but to gain an acceptance of who you are, as you are physically and mentally.

If you experience any discomfort at any stage during the practice, such as muscles tensing up or any feelings of tightness, heaviness or numbness, rather than resisting, try to open to it, imagining the breath travelling there. Regarding the obsessive-compulsive tendencies that Asperger's syndrome can present, this can be a useful exercise in being able to notice how thoughts, feelings and moods can originate from within. Rather than pushing them away or becoming attached to them, it helps to acknowledge them while using the breath as an anchor.

During the practice, you may wish to have your eyes open or closed at various stages. Notice any differences in feelings or sensations when eyes are opened or closed. If you feel any tension, aches and pains, a useful technique is to imagine that the breath can reach wherever it is you feel the discomfort, so as to acknowledge it. Then gradually transfer attention to an area of the body where you feel more comfortable, maintaining your focus on the breath, to gain an appreciation of the interconnectedness of the body.

CHAPTER 7

MANAGING SENSORY ISSUES THROUGH MINDFULNESS

How to Notice Where Autism-related Sensory Issues Influence Thought Patterns by Opening to Them

After practising meditation for quite some time, we become more aware of a wide range of bodily sensations that we are so often oblivious to in life away from practice. Like our emotions, our sensory functions also communicate our needs. Where this can be an issue with Asperger's syndrome is through the narrow fixation tendencies that the condition presents. This chapter explores the relationship between Asperger's syndrome and the sensory functions, looking at how they interlink body and mind, before looking at practice exercises to open up to sensory experiences, including those we may find difficult to cope with.

Many meditation and mindfulness practices are undertaken with the eyes closed. When the eyes are closed during practice and our attention is focused on the breath and bodily sensation, we may realise just how little we make use of some of the sensory functions beyond practice. We may also notice just how tired the ones that we rely on, particularly the eyes, can become at certain times of the day.

Sensory difficulty is an aspect of Asperger's syndrome, high-functioning autism and related conditions that is often ignored. People on the autistic spectrum may experience sensory difficulties in relation to:

- sight
- taste
- touch
- sound
- smell
- bodily feeling.

How people on the autistic spectrum are affected by sensory issues is often individual, largely relating to personal tastes, preferences and perceptions. In various personal accounts and autobiographies written by people on the autistic spectrum, there are often descriptions of difficulties with bright lights and loud noises. Though many people not on the autistic spectrum also have dislike of such issues, more people on the autistic spectrum find it very difficult to cope with such issues because, acting on their autistic tendencies, their natural instinct is to resist by reacting. This can easily be mistaken for bad behaviour.

Suggested coping methods relating to autism and sensory issues tend to focus on strategies to avoid exposure to sensory difficulties, such as avoiding noisy crowds where possible (e.g. doing shopping online rather than going to a crowded shopping centre), or use of alternatives to what they experience as difficulties, such as substitute foods (e.g. alternative textures/flavours to those they have sensory issues with). Such measures are often necessary, certainly for the more rigid individual on the autistic spectrum and in some cases for biological reasons (e.g. needing a gluten-free diet). But what is not often apparent is how, rather than resisting or avoiding where we encounter sensory difficulties, when we open up to different sensory experiences we can become much more in tune with how our experience actually is, in its fullness. Such an approach can enable those of us on the autistic spectrum not only to cope with sensory difficulties, but also to open up to and be with different experiences in the present. Opening up to different sensory experiences can also allow us to get in touch with our sensory functions, particularly those that we may be often oblivious too.

Though we are often aware of what our favourite sensory experiences are, such as our favourite food, sound, clothing material or cosmetics, what is often not so apparent to us is their wider influence on our body and mind. Relating to narrow fixation tendencies that people on the autistic spectrum often have, such influences can become very clearly defined, not only with sensory preferences but also with the thought processes that we may display. Quite often, thought processes can be determined by our sensory likes and dislikes, which can in turn determine our actions. Though it is natural for anyone to have likes and dislikes, whether on the autistic spectrum or not, if we become very rigid with such sensory preferences, we can tend to judge our experiences in relation to them and subsequently become controlled by them.

Though as a person with Asperger's syndrome I have never felt that I have had profound sensory difficulties, I have had difficulties with certain sensory experiences, including noisy and crowded environments. At one time, my natural way of dealing with these was to avoid such situations. With mindfulness, though, I have found that when experiencing such issues, I am able to filter out much of what I find difficult just through being able to notice other sensory functions, as well as being able to adapt to them as they occur. Additionally, I also feel that a more mindful approach has helped to reduce worry as to how I may or may not cope in unpredictable situations that are perhaps new to me, opening me up to the experience as it is.

The two practice exercises described below are to help develop an awareness of different sensory experiences, including how they are interconnected with body and mind. The exercises allow us to open to sensory experiences by holding them in awareness.

Coping: Gong/singing bowl meditation

The purpose of this practice is to develop mindfulness of different sounds, through noticing and opening up to them. For this practice, you would use either a gong or a Tibetan singing bowl. A Tibetan singing bowl is a type of bell shaped like a bowl made from a mixture of different metals that vibrate to produce a smooth, often soothing, ringing sound when the rim is rubbed with a leather-wrapped wooden stick.

When attempting this practice, particularly if for the first time, a Tibetan singing bowl isn't necessary. The exercise can be practised with just about any musical instrument or item that makes a sustained sound when struck or plucked such as a bell, xylophone, triangle or cymbal.

Gongs and Tibetan singing bowls are traditionally used in Buddhism to signal the start and finish of a meditation session. For this exercise, though, the purpose of using a sound is to establish awareness of the sound, including being aware of the sound made at each stage, from the beginning of the sound when the gong is struck or when the singing bowl is rubbed, to when it slowly fades and eventually disappears.

Step 1: This practice is perhaps best done sitting on the floor with your gong, singing bowl or other instrument in front of you. Start by focusing on the breath for a few minutes. As with other practices described in this book, if you notice the mind wandering, just bring attention back to the breath. Now start to focus your attention on sensations you can feel around the ears.

Step 2: Start the sound aspect of the practice by rubbing the rim of the singing bowl or gently striking the gong or other chosen instrument. Make this a part of the meditation rather than a prelude to starting the exercise. Once you have established a sound, gently close your eyes and focus your attention on the sound. Be present with the sound for its duration until you can no longer hear it, possibly including any sensations that you can notice from the sound and its vibrations.

Step 3: Once you can no longer hear the sound, focus awareness on other sounds that you can hear in the absence of the sound of the instrument, including noticing different sounds arising and passing. You may find some sounds to be pleasant (e.g. birds singing) or some to be irritating or perhaps overwhelming (e.g. car engines, machines). Additionally, there may also be some sounds present that affect any sensory difficulties you experience with sound in relation to your condition.

Step 4: When you feel that you are able to hold sounds around you in full awareness, including those that you like and those you dislike, notice your tendency to put labels on what you like and dislike. Now open up to whatever the experience of the practice is, as it is, without judging, before finishing the practice.

Coping: Standing meditation

There are many sensory experiences that are with us constantly, but that we are rarely in tune with. They can often be noticed in postures that we don't assume very often, including standing still for a sustained period of time as in this exercise. The exercise is best practised during a time and in a place where you can be on your own. How long you would like to practise the exercise for is up to you. This can be in accordance with your mental and physical capabilities and limitations, including how long you feel you can stand still for without too much strain, and how long you feel you need to experience the effects of the practice.

Step 1: Start the practice by standing with the arms down the sides, the feet slightly apart and the back straight. Once established in your standing posture, gently close your eyes and start the practice by focusing on the breath. Remember, if you notice that the mind starts to wander, just gently bring your attention back to the breath.

Step 2: Once you feel that your attention is established on the breath, now you can use the breath to expand your awareness throughout the body, including bodily sensations, starting from the soles of the feet and their contact with the floor. Then, gradually work your way up the body, to the ankles, the legs, before moving up to the thighs and around the waist and the backside.

Step 3: While standing, you may start to notice strain in the soles of the feet from supporting the body in an upright position, as well as strain in the calves. Your natural tendency may be to move out of such a position. In relation to autistic or Asperger tendencies, you may engage in a repetitive movement or action as an automatic way of coping. During the practice, though, try to open to any feelings of strain as well as any other bodily feelings that you happen to notice by imagining the breath travelling there, almost like breathing into any areas of strain.

Step 4: Now start to move up to the chest area, then around the upper back before moving up to the shoulders and then down the arms, the hands and fingers before transferring attention to the neck area, around the back of the head, to the scalp and forehead, before moving to the face, each time imagining if the whole body could breathe.

Step 5: Start now to bring attention to any sensory feelings that you can notice within your personal space. Perhaps notice how certain areas of the body feel warmer or cooler in relation to the temperature of the room you are practising in. Notice the air spaces between the fingers, or, if standing barefoot, notice the air space in between the toes, air passing in and out while focusing on the breath coming in and out. Also notice air moving in and out of the spaces between the arms and the body and between the legs and any sensations that it brings.

Step 6: Next, transfer attention to sensations that you can feel on and within the body from the clothes that you are wearing. Notice how the texture of the material you are wearing feels on your skin, including perhaps differences in thicker, heavier materials such as denim and lighter materials such as cotton. Also notice the difference in sensations between parts of the body covered by clothing and those not, as well as the difference in body temperature due to thicker or lighter clothing material. From this experience, notice tendencies to put labels on materials and textures that you like and dislike.

Naturally, an Asperger mind may have a liking for order and structure, which often sees us develop categories into which we sort and place personal preferences and experiences. But when we notice such tendencies just through being present by applying mindfulness, it opens us up to noticing when we are controlled by such preferences and labels. This can enable us to be open to and be part of the experience as it is, rather than see whatever label we put on an experience or category we put it under.

Throughout the remainder of your day, see if you can notice where your thought processes are influenced by sensory experiences that you have noticed in either of the practices described in this chapter.

CHAPTER 8

OBSESSIONS, HABITS, FIXATIONS AND THOUGHTS
Trapped or in Control?

A key aspect of mindfulness practice is noticing patterns of the mind, including thoughts and ways of thinking that arise and pass, including those perhaps related to Asperger tendencies such as obsessions and fixations. The purpose of mindfulness practices, particularly meditation, though, isn't to 'banish' or 'eliminate' such thoughts, but simply to notice when the mind wanders into such thinking, as this is naturally what minds do.

Obsessive thought is not always a negative thing. For people with Asperger's syndrome it can be a strength when intense interest leads to specialisation in a subject or field. However, we have to be careful not to become trapped in it. This chapter looks at how to become more aware of the patterns of the mind and bring awareness of this into life beyond practice.

Obsessive thought processes follow very different, individual, patterns in different people with Asperger's syndrome. Some examples of where obsessive thoughts may originate from include:

- Memories – relating to a time or event in one's life where we were happy or had an enjoyable experience relating to special interests; or a negative experience, perhaps relating to the effects or trauma of a difficult event from our past (e.g. bullying at school).

- Fantasies – we may have a list of things that we would like to experience or achieve, both realistic and unrealistic.

- Ideals – how we feel that we would like to be or like the world around us to be, maybe relating to the Asperger tendency to retreat to our own ordered or structured world, or feeling we might be better understood in a different place or society, sometimes called the 'grass is greener syndrome'.

It is natural for these thoughts to arise in both mindfulness practice and within life away from practice, especially when an event in our life triggers a memory, fantasy or ideal. A problem arises when we find ourselves controlled or trapped by thought in such a way that we lose touch with the present. The frustration that can come from wanting the world around us to be a certain way can lead to stress and anxiety.

Though having a good memory is a strength often associated with Asperger's syndrome, it can also be a weakness when we remember the exact details of difficult or unpleasant experiences, including bullying. Obsessive-compulsive tendencies present within the thought processes of a person with Asperger's syndrome can make it very difficult to let go of such thoughts, to the extent that we may become trapped within them and find ourselves acting upon them in the present, sometimes only adding to frustration caused by holding on to such thoughts.

A model often used by counsellors, psychologists and other related professionals, including by mindfulness practitioners, to explain patterns arising out of individual behaviour is 'ABC'. Founded by Aaron T. Beck in 1921, the ABC model breaks down instances of behaviour and origination of thoughts and thought processes in the following way:

- A – Activating event

- B – Behaviour

- C – Consequences.

Where this model can come into play in relation to Asperger's syndrome is with obsessions and fixations, and also emotions. Emotional actions and consequences are often determined by the activating event, with the actions possibly being determined by thoughts triggered by obsessions or fixations. Such activating events can be highly varied, for example:

- Something that someone has said, with a positive statement resulting in an over-excited reaction or an angry or upset reaction to a negative statement.

- Someone's reaction to what we say, which can be unintentional on our part, particularly if our statement is direct or we are comfortable with the truth, telling it as it is but not being aware of how someone else may react to this.

- Disappointments, such as cancelled events or unsuccessful job interviews, inducing upset or angry reactions, so that we become trapped within feelings of rejection.

- Reaction to a sensory issue or difficulty.

- Reactions to news and media triggered by obsessional behaviour, especially if the news will affect us in a negative way.

Following on from the A, B and C can also come a tightening of obsessive thoughts relating to how we have been affected by an activating event to the point where we become trapped and controlled by such thoughts. When such mind traps occur, we may also find ourselves becoming obsessive not just with thoughts but also with habits, including those that are unhelpful or unhealthy. Such behaviours and habits that we can find ourselves trapped in when obsessed with or controlled by negative thoughts, as well as their subsequent effects, may include:

- procrastination (e.g. putting off phone calls, e-mails, tasks/jobs)

- not sleeping well

- comfort eating

- not eating

- mental fatigue.

Not only are we taken out of the present when such negative thoughts become a controlling factor, but also we can cease to be who we are as we are. Noticing when we are slipping into a downward spiral of negative thought and unhelpful habits is the first step towards taking control, before opening up to and facing them, allowing us to make adjustments to our lifestyle to gradually move away from such patterns. The purpose of mindfulness practice is not to repel such thoughts or habits, as this can only lead to further frustration, but rather to work with them, so that we are able to notice when such thoughts arise and allow them to pass. Similarly, mindfulness enables us to notice urges to slip into a particular habit so that we can decide whether to act upon such urges.

From some of the exercises described in this book, we may open up to how posture can influence our state of mind during practice. This helps to reinforce where this occurs in life away from practice. Requirements that we may have within normal life can include assuming a particular posture for extended periods of time, such as:

- sitting upright at a computer screen

- standing at a desk or display

- crouching to access books and documents.

The strain that such postures put on the body can influence our mental state, including our thoughts.

Mindfulness practice helps us to become aware of our thoughts, including their origins, in a non-judgemental way. With patience, we can eventually notice that thoughts, including those influenced by obsessions and fixations, only have the power that we choose to give them by becoming attached to them to the extent that they dictate our actions. Applying mindfulness helps us to notice that our thoughts are merely just thoughts, not necessarily facts, the way things are or the way we are.

Ultimately, the purpose of mindfulness practice isn't to eliminate obsessions, fixations or thoughts, but rather to work with them. The techniques described below, which can be applied to practices described throughout this book, can help enable this.

Coping: Working with obsessions, fixations and thoughts

As a person with Asperger's syndrome, obsessional thought and narrow fixations may be a strong characteristic of how you are affected by your diagnosis. If so, this is how your mind naturally is, as it is. Like the physical body itself, thoughts are neither fixed nor permanent, and only have the power that you give them through a tendency to get lost within them and thus trapped. To enable detachment from such thoughts and gain control during the mindfulness practice exercises described, it may help to try the following steps:

Step 1: When feeling trapped in negative thoughts, try to be kind and non-judgemental towards yourself. As simple as it may sound, much practice and patience is needed. Simply start by noticing tendencies you may have to put negative labels on yourself.

Step 2: If you are feeling low about what the negative labels suggest, you may have a tendency to resist them or push them away. Instead, just simply acknowledge them, by giving them a degree of attention and then overlooking them, allowing them to pass by or fade.

Step 3: Notice where the mind is moving on to memories, both negative and positive. You may find yourself comfortable when in a happier memory and not want to let go of it, but notice this feeling of not wanting to let go, and allow it to rise and pass. Similarly, if you are in a negative memory, you may want to let go of it quickly. But notice the feeling of wanting to let go, again allowing it to rise and pass.

Step 4: Notice where the mind moves on to fantasies. You may experience fantasies as to how you would like to be or how you would like things to be generally. When such fantasies arise, it is natural that you want to hold on to them. Frustration may also be experienced during practice when your fantasies aren't as you are or as it is. But rather than dismiss fantasies and frustrations, just gently acknowledge them, allowing them to arise and pass, accepting yourself as you are, as it is in the moment.

Step 5: Worries may also arise during practice, which may be about pressing issues in the past or present, or about the future. Notice worries as they arise, acknowledge them, without paying excessive attention to them, allowing them to pass. If you find that you are having difficulty letting go of a worry, just gently bring attention back to the breath, allowing worries to slowly pass. Keeping the breath in mind, acknowledge a worry on the in-breath, allow it to be, and let it slowly exit on the out-breath.

Step 6: If you feel that any thoughts which arise during practice are hard to let go of, you may want to try focusing your attention on the practice exercise you are undertaking. If negative thoughts start to become overpowering, just gently focus your attention on the breath or on sensations in and around the body.

Step 7: You may notice physical discomfort within the body. Your natural tendency may be to resist it, but notice the feeling of wanting to resist. Work with the discomfort by imagining the breath travelling there. If discomfort gets excessive to the point that it is painful, gently adjust your posture, making the movement part of the practice, being aware of any adjustments as you make them while letting go of any tension on the out-breath.

Coping: Weaving mindfulness into life outside practice through habit releasing

Certain habits and obsessions can become very controlling, to the extent that they control you rather than you controlling them. To gain control over them, it helps to work with them. Some suggestions for working with habits include:

1. **Watching television/listening to the radio:** It may be the norm, after an exhausting day working or studying, to wind down by switching on the television or the radio regardless of what is on. Or it could be that you watch certain television programmes out of habit or on autopilot. You may not realise it, but you are not tuned in to what you are watching. You may also find that you are falling into a comfort zone, watching or listening to a programme you are not interested in, but just passing the time. If you feel bored, but there aren't any programmes on television or radio that you normally watch or listen to, you may spend time hopping between channels and stations looking for something and then get frustrated when you can't find anything!

   To work with such habits, it helps to tune in to them by making a point of watching or listening to a particular programme, perhaps picking one out from listings that interests you. During the broadcast of a programme you have picked out to watch, focus your attention in on the programme. Once the programme has finished, then notice what you do, or feelings of wanting to do something but not being sure what. You could use time in between programmes to do a mindfulness exercise if you like.

2. **Internet usage:** If you experience social isolation or difficulties with crowded environments, you may have a tendency to rely on electronic communication, including private e-mail and social media, for social interaction. Or you may just surf the internet when feeling bored or tired, randomly looking at different pages/sites. With social lives increasingly being lived within social media such as Facebook and Twitter and social interaction increasingly taking place within Voice over Internet Protocol (VoIP) technologies such as Skype, many people's lives are becoming dominated by such facilities.

Asperger or obsessive-compulsive tendencies may see us experiencing urges to keep checking for messages/notifications. Or, if feeling lonely, we may keep signing into VoIPs to see who we can chat to, possibly becoming frustrated when no friends are online.

Start by noticing tendencies to go online when bored or wanting to fill in time. If you use social media, start noticing any urges to check for messages/notifications. To help work with these habits, before logging on have a purpose in mind, such as to research information for a project. Similarly, before logging onto social media, approach it with a purpose, such as to contact a friend you haven't been in touch with for a while.

You may want to use a diary to record observations on different approaches you apply towards habits. Don't expect old habits to disappear overnight, but instead allow them to dissolve over time, while slowly noticing awareness of and choice over actions that follow habits.

CHAPTER 9

REFRESHING ASPERGER'S SYNDROME

*Expanding Sensory Experience
and Awareness through Practising
Mindfulness of Walking*

When exploring meditation for the first time, we can initially form the preconception that it involves stillness and sitting for long periods of time in a cross-legged posture. When I first started meditation practice, I hadn't realised that it involved more than just sitting, but that there are also practices that involve walking. Walking meditation is a really useful exercise for people with Asperger's syndrome, who find that they perhaps engage repetitive movement or are hyperactive, to develop mindfulness through just noticing movement.

Introducing mindfulness practice to people with Asperger's syndrome, particularly those who have difficulties with high-level anxiety, can sometimes have a reverse effect. The more you try to help them calm down, the more anxious and stressed they can become from trying and not feeling that it is making any difference. Fortunately, though, mindfulness practice is flexible in that it can be effectively adapted to individual needs. Jon Kabat-Zinn (2004) notes how some who have struggled with sitting meditation practice, finding it difficult to sit still for a sustained period of time, have taken to meditation through walking practice. Similarly, by being flexible towards the needs of an individual with Asperger's syndrome, working with their issues or aspects of their behaviour, including repetitive movement, can be an effective way of introducing meditation techniques and related relaxation exercises.

New experiences, like trekking in extreme environments such as the Himalayas or the Andes, can broaden our mind in the sense that we may find out more about ourselves. We may gain a clearer understanding of our strengths and weaknesses as well as how we cope. This often enables small changes to our lifestyle that can make a significant difference or open up an entirely new outlook on life. Trekking in such environments presents different challenges that arise from moment to moment in the changeable micro-climate that mountainous regions create, from dry and dusty lower down to heavy rain and bitterly cold winds which become noticeable when passing the treeline. The constantly changing conditions that mountains bring affect us mentally as much as physically, in the sense that they contribute to feelings and moods. Doubt can creep into the mind as to whether or not we can actually complete the trek and return to the starting point. When doubt enters the mind, we can slip out of the present moment to the extent that we lose touch with the present conditions, which could possibly mean being blown off course by strong winds or slipping on dusty tracks.

When successfully completing a trek, though, after being through a series of ever-changing conditions over a few days, we can feel like we have returned home after spending many years of finding ourselves. Similarly, with the right effort and attention, mindfulness of walking practice can also have this effect. Also, with the right support, an Asperger's syndrome diagnosis can enable us to see who we are in a different light from a refreshed perspective. Even when we have had an Asperger's syndrome diagnosis for some time, though, we can become set in our ways to the extent that our condition controls us. This can mean that we become unaware, and stepping outside our routines can be like stepping into a foreign country or slipping out of the present. To maintain awareness, it is often helpful to step back from the flow so that we can refresh our Asperger's syndrome, including being able to adapt it to the present.

The meditation retreat at the Samatha Centre in Wales involves two guided group sitting practices, one in the morning and one in the evening. Outside this, much of the practice that I have undertaken during meditation retreats has largely been walking practice, both indoors and outdoors. The centre has various footpaths where visitors can practise mindfulness of walking going up a hill and through woodlands. The different routes offer different sensory experiences. While practising on the woodland route, one can notice a change in sensations when coming out of the woodland, in terms of what one is shielded from by the trees, such as wind, sunlight and sometimes rain. When it is raining, the sensations of the rain are more noticeable and can be surprisingly pleasant, allowing one to adapt to the conditions just through opening to them. Normally the very thought of having to walk in rain can induce feelings of frustration or resistance. But just by being able adapt to it by being in the moment with the rain or wind through opening to it can make it a pleasant experience. The experience can also show us how we can sometimes be so presumptuous or irrational in our thinking that we can create our own conditions rather than experiencing and accepting them as they are.

Unlike running a marathon or undertaking a trek to the summit of a mountain, mindfulness of walking practice doesn't have a target or goal to reach and can be practised in any convenient space. Not having such a target can mean less pressure, which allows for more freedom to focus on the actual walking step by step and to notice the difference in sensations with each movement. Also, the advantage of not having a target or goal helps to remove any feelings of doubt about whether we can reach it. Such feelings of doubt can lead to anxiety which can take us out of the present moment.

At first, we may question why meditation practice can be done walking when we may do much walking in life beyond practice. Often, though, when walking in normal life, we do it as part of our daily routine or on autopilot. Mindfulness of walking practice, however, is a good way to come out of autopilot mode as described in Chapter 1. Also, following on from Chapter 7, which looks at getting in touch with sensory experience, mindfulness of walking practice offers a way to expand this awareness as it is a multi-sensory activity, adding movement to awareness of bodily sensations. This helps in noticing the differences in sensations affected by each step during the walk. If the walk is practised outdoors, it helps us notice the changes in weather conditions and temperature that affect bodily sensations and thoughts. Particularly noticeable when walking in wind or rain is the difference in sensations when wearing a hat or hood, as opposed to being bare-headed, and the different thoughts and moods influenced by different sensations.

Personally, I have found that practising mindfulness of walking has added an extra dimension to being present as well as enabling me to step back from the flow effectively. I feel that it has also made it possible for me to return to life outside practice with a refreshed approach. This helps me to avoid having too many expectations and assumptions as to what the next moments might be, enabling me to handle and experience things on a moment-to-moment basis, as well as not become too controlled by feelings of doubt and uncertainty.

The following practice, mindfulness of walking, offers you an opportunity to expand your sensory awareness and to notice just how much you may operate on autopilot in normal life, as well as to return to normal life with a refreshed outlook.

Coping: Mindfulness of walking practice

This is a practice that can be undertaken in any convenient space, both indoors and outdoors. A mindfulness of walking exercise can be practised walking in a straight line or in a circle. Remember that the practice is about the walk and being present with the sensations of each step, so avoid setting any targets or goals for where you are going to walk to.

How long you practise this exercise and how far you walk depends on your physical capabilities and limitations. It can also depend on how much physical space is available for you in which to practise or, if you are practising outside, your tolerance levels of different weather conditions. The practice can be done wearing shoes or barefoot. If barefoot, you can gain a stronger notice of sensations from the contact of the foot with the ground.

Step 1: Start the practice by standing still, with the arms by the sides. Prior to starting the walking part of the practice, it helps to gain awareness both of the breath and of sensations, as you will hold these in awareness during the walk. Slowly start to focus your attention on the breath using a length of breath that you feel comfortable with. Notice the sensations of the in-breath coming in through the nose and going down through the lungs to the diaphragm. Also notice how the chest expands outwards on the in-breath and how it contracts inwards on the out-breath. If you feel the mind wandering, just bring your attention back to the breath.

Step 2: Once you feel that your attention is established on the breath, start to notice sensations in the soles of the feet from the contact with the ground before slowly working your way up the body until you feel you are fully present within the body as a whole.

Step 3: Before starting the walking, focus on the ground immediately in front of you. Now start by slowly lifting your left foot and taking a step forward before placing the foot in front of you. Once the left foot is firmly on the ground, repeat the movement with your right foot, continuing the following sequence:

- lifting
- moving
- placing.

If you are walking in a straight line back and forth, make the turning during the change of direction a part of the practice, rather than a break, being aware of the same sequence of movements.

Step 4: During the walking practice, notice the sensations involved in each movement from the foot lifting, to the foot off the ground, to the falling and then the placing of the foot, while simultaneously holding awareness of the breath. Notice where you start doing the practice on autopilot once fully engaged in the sequence. In particular, you may notice that you start lifting your feet without being aware of the movement. But don't worry, as it is natural to become set within a movement or comfort zone, especially in relation to Asperger tendencies. However, it is helpful that you are able to notice this during the practice.

Step 5: After you have been doing the practice for a sustained period of time, you can start to expand your awareness from the ground upwards to the space you are walking in. If you are practising outside, notice the varying effects that factors such as wind, light and temperature can have on your movement and on sensations, fully aware of each movement in each moment.

Step 6: As this practice has a multi-sensory dimension to it, in that you are noticing the breath while noticing sensations from ongoing physical movement, it may initially take a few attempts to notice and experience its effects beyond practice. To see the benefits of this practice in normal life, it helps not to have any expectations about any changes that it will bring. Instead, just allow any noticing and awareness that you develop during practice to gradually unfold over time, with practice refreshing your experience of existence within your surroundings.

CHAPTER 10

STEERING THE RAFT THROUGH THE SOCIAL WORLD

You Can't Control the Social Flow, but You Can Adapt Your Asperger's Syndrome to It

Located on New Zealand's South Island is the Rangitata River, one of the braided rivers that make up the Canterbury Plains and a popular place to participate in white-water rafting. Surrounded by mountains, the river and landscape bring their own ever-changing conditions that contribute to the experience of white-water rafting from moment to moment – rather like how the changing effects of Asperger's syndrome contribute to life experience as it unfolds within different phases and through life's ups and downs. Gently rowing through calmer, more steadily flowing parts of the river one moment, before holding on to the raft when being pulled down by rapids the next, requires different modes of attention and coping. In this sense, the journey can almost be analogous to one's whole life condensed into the space of a few hours.

A Maori word, the name Rangitata has been variously translated as 'day of lowering clouds', 'close sky' and 'side of the sky', referring to the thick mists that the river brings which can obscure the route for rafters. Often, different weather conditions are reflected in human moods and emotions. When conditions are cloudy and misty, we may feel that our thoughts and emotions are confused, in the sense that we may feel that we don't know where we are or where we are going because we can't see through the mist. But when conditions turn sunny and clear, blue skies are uncovered, and visibility is clearer, we may feel more assured. Different weather conditions also have different effects on bodily feeling and sensations. We can feel constrained by colder, wetter conditions but may feel more freedom in warmer conditions. Such feelings can often contribute to our changing thoughts and moods, influencing our behaviour and actions when we are least aware. Changing weather conditions are almost like the location, the river and its mountainous surroundings, expressing its emotions.

As the location expresses its emotions, the flow of the rapids takes us to where we find ourselves. The river controls us in the same way that we are controlled by our thoughts, stresses and anxieties. Along the river banks, though, are 'eddies', calm spots where water gathers behind rocks, shielded from the flow. Rafters are encouraged to swim to an eddy if they fall out of the raft so that they are not caught in the rapids. Just as eddies can offer respite for the stranded rafter, mindfulness practice can offer us a way to step back from the flow of the social world, as well as from the stresses and anxieties that the flow of life can present. To people with Asperger's syndrome, triggers of stress and anxiety that we may find very difficult to cope with often include uncertainty over the future beyond college/ university, coping with uncertainty over a career, or any situations that we have not yet experienced where we feel that our condition may negatively affect us.

Coping with the different effects that different conditions bring often requires different approaches and techniques, which we have to adjust to. When going through rapids, rafters usually have to adjust from rowing to hanging on and jumping down into the raft to avoid falling out or the raft capsizing. Being able to recognise effects or consequences of our own actions, especially where they affect others, is very difficult for many people with Asperger's syndrome. By not reacting quickly enough when going down rapids, one could fall out of the raft and find oneself left behind or the raft could capsize and the whole crew fall out. It is often only in the event of this happening that a person with Asperger's syndrome begins to realise their interconnections with others around them, including consequences of actions.

In a social situation, many people with Asperger's syndrome can feel that non-verbal communication is hidden behind a smokescreen. Not being able to see the route ahead can present us with confusion and anxiety over how to cope with the next moment as it unfolds. When white-water rafting with an experienced instructor who encourages the crew to treat the raft as their 'lifejacket' and who knows the rapids well, one feels assured. In many social situations, though, a person with Asperger's syndrome doesn't have a non-verbal communication interpreter to explain the unwritten rules of non-verbal social interaction as it occurs. Thus, difficulties with understanding non-verbal communication can be a trigger of anxiety for those of us with Asperger's syndrome. We may be unsure as to how others feel about us, especially if we find that we desire friendships.

Different sections and grades of rapids present different challenges during a white-water rafting excursion. Similarly, as with people not on the autistic spectrum, different stages in the lives of people with Asperger's syndrome throw up different challenges. Often, though, for many people with the condition, it can sometimes affect how we cope with, respond to and adapt to different life stages. This includes coming out of childhood into adolescence, before moving into adulthood and independent living. During different life phases, we need to develop different relationships, which often require new sets of emotions as well as different social skills.

Just like one's natural instinct when rafting through strong currents may be to try to row away from or avoid the current, the natural tendency of a person with Asperger's syndrome may be to avoid social situations. With mindfulness, though, we often begin to realise that it is our own thoughts and emotions that can detract from how the situation actually is. Resistance often only causes more problems. When rowing with the current, one has more control over the raft as the raft protects you. Similarly, when those of us with Asperger's syndrome open up to socialisation, we can develop skills, perhaps through observation, to mask aspects of our condition so that we can function effectively around others. With development of mindfulness, together with observation and with practice, such masking techniques can be developed. Just like the raft is used to help steer us down the rapids, being able to mask our Asperger characteristics enables us to steer through the social world. Once a white-water rafting excursion is finished, the raft is stored away in a garage or shed for further excursions. After a person with Asperger's syndrome leaves a social situation to go home or spend time alone, that person can take off their social mask.

Despite efforts that I have made, as well as the efforts made by other individuals diagnosed with Asperger's syndrome, to raise awareness of Asperger's syndrome through public speaking, what I feel I have learned is that we cannot stop or even change the flow of the social world. But we can adapt the way we are in relation to our Asperger's syndrome to cope with the challenges that the social flow can present. Mindfulness practice, I feel, has enabled me to step back from the flow of the social world, allowing me to observe it and my relationship with it. There are aspects of the social world that will present challenges and trigger stresses and anxieties. With development of mindfulness, though, I have found that I am able to adapt to the ever-changing social flow more effectively through changing my relationship to it, rather than resisting it or hiding from it.

Stress and anxiety are often intrinsic to our life and manifest in various shapes and forms and from various triggers. Resisting stressful situations only causes further anxiety, while hiding from them can lead to social isolation, which for many people with Asperger's syndrome, including myself, can lead to depression. Qualities developed during mindfulness practice, though, when applied to situations beyond practice, can enable us to change our relationship to triggers of stress and anxiety to the extent that we can work with them.

Being able to work with stress and anxiety through being with it as it unfolds from moment to moment can open us up to new experiences, including being able to enjoy the thrills of various activities and exercises. Far from being confined to practice, mindfulness can be developed and applied effectively within different situations and experiences, thus tuning us in to the experience as it unfolds, enriching our lives.

Coping: Applying mindfulness to experiences in daily life beyond practice

Beyond the mindfulness practice exercises described in this book, opportunities to practise mindfulness are not just confined to activities which we may consider daring or exciting, such as white-water rafting, climbing or sky-diving. Even tasks and duties that we may consider to be routine or mediocre are often good opportunities to practise and apply mindfulness:

> If mindfulness is deeply important to you, then every moment is an opportunity to practise. (Jon Kabat-Zinn 2004, p.77)

Just about every moment of our life can present opportunities to both practise and apply mindfulness. Below are some examples of where mindfulness can be applied in daily life.

1. **Physical exercise:** Often recommended as a way of coping with depression and low self-esteem as well as developing physical fitness and stamina, exercise is a really good opportunity to practise mindfulness. A useful starting point in applying mindfulness for physical exercise is not to think of an exercise or workout as a competition. You are not undertaking the activity in competition with yourself or anybody else. Being able to acknowledge your physical capabilities and limitations also helps, so that you are able to undertake a workout that challenges you but that you can manage. For instance, when lifting weights, it helps to use a weight that isn't necessarily light or too easy to lift, but neither is it so heavy that you are straining to lift it. During your exercise, in different activities, try tuning in your awareness to sensations in the body parts involved in the exercise, including differences between sensations in parts involved in the exercise and parts that are not.

2. **Eating and drinking:** As part of the eight-week mindfulness-based stress reduction course, participants are given a mindful eating exercise. The exercise involves eating raisins as slowly as possible, to enable one to notice the taste, flavour and texture. Feedback from many participants suggests that however much we eat and drink, we rarely taste and experience its full flavour. This is largely because we are not in the moment while we eat and drink. When eating or drinking, where possible try taking some time to open yourself up to the taste, flavour and texture by being with it. If you like the taste, try not to become attached to it, or if you dislike the taste, rather than resist it (which may involve spitting it out!), open to it. Notice also your tendencies to put labels on tastes, flavours and textures you like and dislike.

3. **Washing the dishes:** When undertaking this task, your tendency may be to rush through it to get it out of the way, especially if it is seen as a hindrance to having time to do other things, including perhaps to undertake a meditation practice. When we rush tasks, even those we see as routine or mediocre, we are not in the moment. When doing the washing up, try opening up to sensations of the water and detergent on your hands, contact with the dishcloth or sponge and the dishes themselves, including noticing differences between different dishes. Also you may notice perhaps where the mind wanders, possibly thinking about what you may otherwise like to be doing! Each time this happens, gently focus attention back on where you are in the moment with your task. Just simply noticing where the mind wanders is applying mindfulness.

4. **Brushing your teeth:** It is known that some individuals on the autistic spectrum have sensory issues with the effect of the toothbrush bristles on their teeth. As this is something that we do on a regular basis, we tend to develop routine ways

of doing it to the extent that it becomes a habit, for example starting in the same place each time. When we get set in such habits, we may either pay little attention or miss other parts. Over a period of four to five days, when brushing your teeth try starting in a different place each time. When doing so, notice any differences you feel in the place that you have brushed and the places that you haven't yet covered. If you experience sensory difficulties with toothbrush bristles, rather than trying to push away or filter out such feeling, it may help to open to it and acknowledge it, just through noticing the contact of the toothbrush on the teeth and gums.

5. **Taking a shower:** Again, taking a shower may seem like a routine part of your day that doesn't change. During a shower, we may be focused on what we are planning to do throughout our day, to the extent that we are taken out of the present. To tune in to the present while taking a shower, try simply just noticing the sensations of the contact of the water with your hair and skin, as well as the texture of the soap and shampoo you are using. When turning off the shower, notice the difference in sensations between contact with running water and non-contact with running water, perhaps including the difference in temperature. When drying, notice the texture of the towel on your skin, as well as sensory differences between your skin being wet and then dry.

6. **Having a conversation:** Many people diagnosed with Asperger's syndrome may be the first to admit that they are not the most natural of conversationalists. They may also have a tendency to shy away from a conversation due to feelings of being unsure of what to talk about. Alternatively, others with Asperger's syndrome may feel confident in a conversation if they feel as though they have opinions to express or knowledge to offer. What may not be obvious to them in the latter case is that

the person they are talking to may become bored if they are talking in too much detail about a special interest! During a conversation, notice where this happens and perhaps also, where possible, notice facial expression, which may suggest that the person you are talking to is bored. Also, notice how your talking affects your own body language and facial expression. If someone wants to start a conversation with you, it may help to apply the attention and concentration levels that you have experienced during mindfulness practice, enabling you to be able to listen mindfully, not just to the words spoken, but also to how they are spoken.

7. **In the workplace:** Depending on the type of work you do, how you may be able to apply mindfulness to working situations is highly varied. You may find in a working situation that you have a list of tasks to do, some of which you are either unsure about or not comfortable with that you may procrastinate over, for example making phone calls to strangers. If this occurs, notice where procrastination causes delay, especially if you have to meet deadlines. Then notice where delay creates further uncertainty that can lead to stress and anxiety, to the extent that you are driven from the present. Where this happens, just gently focus the mind back onto the tasks in hand, by being present with each stage of the task through to completion.

The above suggestions are neither comprehensive nor exhaustive. See if they fit into your life. Or you may find other situations you experience on a regular basis to which you can bring mindfulness, for example studying, reading, driving, playing a musical instrument or listening to music. In each case, open to any sensations experienced through touch or bodily feeling and notice where the mind wanders. Don't worry if this happens, as minds naturally wander. Each time you notice this happen, though, just gently bring the mind back to focus on what you are doing in the present.

Due to your Asperger tendencies, you may feel that you undertake different tasks and duties, including those described above, out of routine, to the extent that they appear or feel the same each time. With mindfulness, however, you may notice that each experience of washing dishes or brushing your teeth is different, rather like each breath during a meditation practice is different in terms of length and sensations experienced.

CHAPTER 11

MINDFULNESS AND QUALITY OF LIFE

How I Feel that Mindfulness Has Enabled Me to Tune in to the Here and Now through Applying Equanimity

One of the first things that I feel I have found out about myself in relation to my Asperger's syndrome is what I am good at – worrying! Just through noticing how this particular tendency plays on my mind has enabled me to see the effects that it can have on my actions in each moment of my day. In the broader spectrum, it has opened me up to how my life unfolds. The awareness that I have developed from continuous mindfulness practice in both a spiritual and a secular context I also feel has enabled me to bring about and apply equanimity to my life as it unfolds. This has helped me with my mental stability.

The term equanimity, originating from the Latin *aequanimitas* meaning 'even mind', refers to a state of mental or emotional stability or composure arising from a deep awareness and acceptance of the present moment. Such a deep awareness and acceptance of the way it is, whatever the circumstances, enables freedom for us to actually be in the present, rather than be controlled by tendencies, including those related to Asperger's syndrome.

To find such freedom, though, it is helpful to start just by noticing the effects that Asperger-related tendencies described throughout this book can have on our relationship with the present. To notice these effects, it helps to gain an understanding of who you are to enable you to see how you relate to the presence of your surroundings. This can be enabled by understanding your mental and physical capabilities and limitations as well as understanding personal strengths and weaknesses you may have because of your Asperger's syndrome. Understanding ourselves in this way when held together in awareness of the present helps us to understand and anticipate how each moment unfolds as we experience it.

Being diagnosed with Asperger's syndrome can bring much uncertainty both in terms of the confusion it can create in understanding who you are socially, as well as how you relate to others around you. It can also be equally confusing as to how others relate to you and also with the anxiety and stress that such confusion can bring. Confusion often brings about thoughts that can cloud our mind. In relation to obsessive tendencies that we may have, this can lead us to holding on to thoughts. The uncertainty that comes with the confusion can also lead us to believing in our thoughts to the extent that we think they are real.

For many people with Asperger's syndrome, including myself, this confusion and uncertainty can lead to a feeling of not being understood within reality, and we may withdraw into a special interest or obsession or into our own, often imaginative, fantasy worlds. Though this can be an effective way of coping up to a point, we have to be careful that we don't end up becoming cut off from both the social world and the outside world generally. This can happen if we become attached to our thoughts or imaginary world to the extent that it becomes difficult to let go. Such tendencies are far from unique to people on the autistic spectrum. According to the respected Buddhist Monk Ajahn Chah (2007), as human beings we have a tendency to 'build walls' around ourselves. This can mean that the world we often find ourselves living in becomes constrained by the wall that is our thoughts and perceptions, which can be very different to how things actually are.

Naturally, it is difficult for many people with Asperger's syndrome to understand the perspectives and perceptions of others. Added to this, understanding how our own perspectives, perceptions, presentation and actions affect others may also be difficult. Rigid thought patterns and feelings of low self-esteem that can arise from social isolation begin to control the mind to the extent that we become trapped by them. This can lead to our activities and actions becoming dictated by our thoughts and perception. In accordance with my own personal experiences of Asperger's syndrome, I have often found myself avoiding or walking away from social situations due to feelings of inadequacy, through not being able to match up to others or relate to topics of conversation. With mindfulness, I have since begun to understand that shutting myself off from the social world not only creates more anxiety and low self-esteem, but is also unhelpful for social development. As well as limiting opportunities to develop social skills and make social connections, avoidance of such situations can also be a factor in developing preconceptions which can lead to one becoming judgemental.

In a working environment, uncertainty created by such feelings can become a hindrance not just in expressing issues and concerns. It can also be a hindrance to expressing our ideas and encourages procrastination over tasks or activities. In many working situations, if we are feeling controlled by feelings of low self-esteem or lack of confidence, we may find ourselves putting off tasks, especially if we have to contact others to undertake them.

Where I first started to notice the effects of being tuned in to the present was when starting a new job working as Operational Manager in software testing at Autism Works, a social enterprise which offers sustainable employment to people on the autistic spectrum. As well as there being a lot for me to learn regarding new duties, responsibilities and general working practices, there were also many practices that I felt had become ingrained into me from previous posts that I had to unlearn. Naturally, as a person with Asperger's syndrome, change isn't easy for me to come to terms with or to adapt to. But I found that by being tuned in to the present and where I was in each moment in starting my new role, I found it much easier to concentrate on tasks in hand, including making phone calls to people with whom I was not familiar.

With mindfulness, we may find that when tuned in to the way it is here and now in the present, our relationship with the world can become much clearer and we can see that our thoughts are not facts and our perception is different from reality. By making our relationship with our surroundings, both physical and social, more intimate we enable ourselves to notice our interconnections with more clarity. For when we become isolated by our thoughts and perceptions, we tend to see the world around us from an isolated perspective, almost like being in a bubble or ivory tower. Because we are not immediately aware of how what goes on outside our bubble directly affects us, we can be vulnerable to stress and anxiety resulting from unexpected changes in circumstances or appear blind to the consequences of our actions. It can take quite some effort to understand this, especially for an individual with Asperger's syndrome who naturally struggles with being able to understand the consequences of their own actions as well as the actions of others.

However, an aspect of the Asperger mind that can enable us to see our interconnections is visual thinking. Many people with Asperger's syndrome find links very helpful. Different moments throughout our day, week, month, year and, in the broader spectrum, throughout our lifetime rarely unfold in isolation. They are usually the results of our interconnections. In reverse, our actions and, in many ways, our very livelihoods are often determined by the actions of others and reliance on others to the point where we are largely interdependent on one another.

The monastic lifestyle in Buddhism teaches us much about the value of interdependence. As Buddhist monks are unable to handle money due to their precepts, they can't go out to the supermarket to buy their food. They have to rely on the lay community to provide them with their food and upkeep in the form of alms donations, in return for teachings, help and guidance. This makes it important for monastic communities to maintain good relations with the lay community. Similarly, a software testing company needs contracts from software developers who need their products to be well-tested. In turn, software developers need customers to sell their products to, while customers need software products for their livelihood, for both business and recreational purposes. Such interdependence, which results from interconnections, also shows us the need for good working and personal relations. When practising mindfulness, as well as when writing, speaking or giving training on Asperger's syndrome, I have found awareness of interdependence helpful in being able to notice the link between the effects of mindfulness and the tendencies of Asperger's syndrome, including how they are interconnected.

Mindfulness practice is an available and accessible route towards taking away much of the confusion that we may experience between our thoughts and perceptions and reality, as well as enabling us to distinguish between thoughts and awareness. For people with Asperger's syndrome it can be, with the right effort, a route towards gaining control over the tendencies that our condition presents, liberating us from being controlled by them. Mindfulness also helps us to develop and apply equanimity, through simply being aware of how we actually are as individuals and how we are affected by Asperger's syndrome, as opposed to what we are not or what we would ideally like to be. Equanimity developed through mindfulness also enables acceptance of how we are in relation to the present moment, including being accepting of the present moment as it is rather than as we would ideally like it to be.

The practice activities described throughout this book focus on being able to acknowledge thoughts, including those that are positive, negative or neutral, allowing us to let thoughts arise and pass without becoming attached to them. Whichever practice you are undertaking, though, if you find that you feel lost in – or maybe even preoccupied by – your thoughts, don't worry, as this is human nature. But just being able to notice when this occurs is a helpful starting point towards detachment from being controlled by your thought processes. This enables awareness of the sources of your thoughts as they arise and pass, thus being able to notice if you are stuck in the past or becoming over-anxious about the future. Such a feeling of detachment can enable you to switch off effectively from any pressures or constraints you may feel are present in life, before facing them from a neutral and more refreshed perspective by applying equanimity. With this level of awareness and understanding, you can gain more freedom to experience the richness of being with, rather than being controlled by, your condition in the present.

Personally, I have found that wherever I go and whatever I do, my past, present and future are with me, as well as is my Asperger's syndrome. Just by being able to tune all these and other factors in to the present, being with them here and now, I am much more at ease with myself, knowing my capabilities and limitations mentally and physically. I feel this has given me more freedom to be here and now in the present, with each moment as it unfolds.

Figure 11.1 shows the interconnections between mindfulness practice, noticing thought patterns, tuning in to the present moment and equanimity. In accordance with the theme of this book, the diagram doesn't represent a concrete path to improvement in quality of life. From an Asperger's syndrome perspective, though, many people, including myself, consider themselves to be largely visual thinkers. Thus, an image or a diagram is helpful to illustrate what is being talked or written about, and also to see the links. The purpose of the diagram, rather than show a route to an improvement in quality of life, or indeed equanimity, is to show how different aspects of mindfulness practice interrelate. It is up to you to find a route towards experiencing your potential qualities, to find a route that suits your individual needs, though guidance can help point the way.

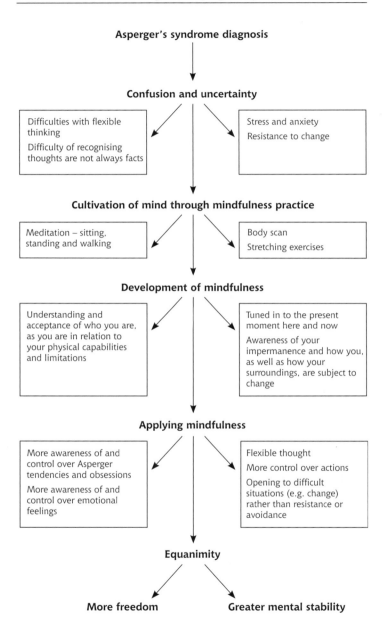

Figure 11.1 Pathway to equanimity from an Asperger's syndrome diagnosis

CHAPTER 12

PLEASE DON'T RUSH!
Finding Flow Here and Now

Though the theme of this book is about being here and now in the present, there is much that we can learn from the past on the theme of time, which can be effectively applied to the present and to mindfulness practice itself. At Rufford Old Hall, a sixteenth-century house in Cheshire, England, there is an example of a lantern clock, an early mechanical clock. At first observation it appears to be a standard clock. But on closer inspection, the visitor will notice that it only has one hand, an hour hand and no minute hand. This difference isn't often immediately noticed by the visitor because on autopilot we immediately assume from a distance that a clock has at least two hands. Also, in contemporary times we are much more time-conscious, driven by much more precise times than we were in the past, when time was much more flexible. Priorities in what was then a largely agrarian society were much more dependent on seasons and conditions.

Various tasks and activities we pursue in the modern world, from simple tasks such as making a cup of tea to longer-term tasks or projects such as writing a book, involve allocating a certain amount of time. It could be from a few minutes to several hours, or it may extend to a few days or several weeks. As well as allocating time, in the contemporary world we can also find ourselves becoming heavily reliant on precise timings for public transport and opening and closing times of places of business.

Timekeeping, from natural forms using the sun and moon to human conventions of time using dates, calendars and mechanical clocks, has very visible effects on human behaviour, as well as on consciousness.

Visiting Laos, in South East Asia, economically one of the world's poorest nations, a visitor from the developed world is immediately taken out of their comfort zone seeing not just the dramatic differences in lifestyles, but also how slow-paced a society it feels. As well as seeing what many Laotians don't have in material terms, for example technology and modern appliances that are often the norm for the visitor from the developed world, one also sees much of what we have lost in the developed world, including how we have largely lost touch with a natural pace of life. The official name of Laos is the Lao People's Democratic Republic (PDR), though Laotians like to say that PDR also stands for 'please don't rush'. This is evident in how, even in the capital city Vientiane, shops and places of business still largely open and close at their convenience, without the rush around the clock to open up stores or any rush to get to the shops as soon as they open.

In the developed world, meanwhile, life is driven by so many different factors, not just our concept of time but also technological innovations we take for granted. Factors that put us on autopilot include immediate access to information online and instant communication via mobile phone calls, text messages, e-mail and, more recently, social networks. Such innovations have contributed to escalating the pace of life and we plan our lives around them to the extent that we often experience difficulties coping when something goes wrong. As well as taking us out of the present, autopilot mode can also create expectations as to how our day, week, month, year or indeed our life may turn out. Similarly, when attempting mindfulness practice for the first time, it may be natural for us to have early expectations or hopes as to how it will help improve our life, especially if we are going through a difficult period personally.

In relation to Asperger tendencies, as explained throughout this book, it is very understandable that people with the condition like to have a routine to enable predictability to avoid excessive stress in dealing with unpredictable situations or having to adapt to unforeseen circumstances that may occur in our perceived future. Difficulties in understanding social interactions and social motives can also contribute to problems with being able to anticipate such circumstances, for example cancellations of events or activities due to personal circumstances, either one's own or those of others involved. The routine-orientated nature of a person with Asperger's syndrome may also mean a liking for the more visible and largely structured nature of clock or calendar time, with difficulties in understanding the more abstract and much less apparent nature of natural or organic time.

Experiencing different perceptions of time, whether it is sixteenth-century English time or present-day Laotian time, involves coming out of our comfort zone, like mindfulness practice itself. As well as noticing and acknowledging habits we may have when in autopilot mode, coming out of our comfort zone can also help us notice any expectations that we may have in what we expect to happen throughout the course of our day, week, month or even year. Such expectations can also extend to perception of our future, including aspirations and goals. Though aspirations and goals can be a useful motivating factor, we also have to be careful if the goal or aspiration not only takes us out of the present but also creates unrealistic expectations to the extent that we experience a high level of disappointment, leading to depression and low self-esteem.

Similarly, if attempting mindfulness practice for the first time, especially if going through a difficult period, we may have similar expectations that our life is going to change or improve dramatically, courtesy of mindfulness practice, before we have even attempted it. Mindfulness practice can have the reverse effect if we go into it with expectations, as the experience of the practice may be rather different to any initial expectations we may have had. During practice, we can also become lost in such expectations so that we may lose touch with the experience or flow of the practice itself:

> Meditation is like cultivating your garden: your experience deepens and changes, but this takes place in horticultural time, not clock time. (Williams and Penman 2011, p.152)

In addition to expectations, another hindrance to mindfulness practice can be pressure coming from feeling that we have to practise here and now or have to set times around other commitments such as family, work and/ or study. Such pressure can extend to anxiety when we become worried that we haven't practised yet today or that we don't have time or space to practise. Understandably, a person with Asperger's syndrome seeking mindfulness practice may want to have a routine or timetable for when and where to practise meditation or a stretching exercise. Though commitment is often initially needed to start practising on a regular basis, we also have to be careful that we don't become dictated to by the need to practise. This only creates pressure that can result in stress and anxiety.

When starting mindfulness practice, particularly practising for the first time, we also may be unsure as to how long to practise for. This is where the concept of flexible or organic time, rather than scheduled time, can help. If we are used to setting aside time to complete a task or project, it may be in our nature to set aside time to practise mindfulness. If we find a mindfulness practice exercise difficult or uncomfortable, for example experiencing numbness during sitting, strain from stretching or general frustration from negative thoughts taking control, there may be the tendency to keep looking at a watch or clock in front of us to see how long is left of the time that we set aside to practise, or we may simply just break off the exercise. The results of either response can be the reverse of what any initial expectations were.

Psychologist Mihaly Csikszentmihalyi (1998) in his work *Finding Flow* suggests that anxieties are often induced by our daily obligations, including time, which disrupts flow. Examples of where our flow can be disrupted can include when undertaking what we may feel is a mediocre or energy-sapping task so that we become more obsessive about clock-watching to the extent that we may lose focus on the task in hand. When pursuing leisure activities or hobbies, such an obsession with time or progress can also be a flow-disrupting factor. A classic example is when running a marathon: if we are starting to tire, we may become obsessed with how much further we need to go to reach the finish line. Another is in climbing a mountain: how much further it is to the summit. This is where we can become so lost in our goal that it takes us out of the present. To stay present with the task in hand, it helps to focus on doing the run rather than reaching the finish line, or to focus on doing the climb rather than reaching the summit. This approach allows more flow within one's effort. Such approaches can also be applied effectively to mindfulness practice.

Notes for approaching mindfulness practice

If you are new to mindfulness practice:

- Avoid having any preconceptions or expectations about what you think may be the outcomes for you.

- When undertaking a practice exercise, including those described in this book, it may help not to set a time limit as to how long to practise for. Rather, allow the wisdom of your body to let you know when is long enough, or if undertaking a stretching exercise, how far to stretch.

- Don't see yourself as being in competition with either yourself or with others as to how long you can practise for, how long you can hold a posture for, how physically flexible you are or how far you can stretch.

- Though a degree of commitment is needed to practise, especially if you are going to practise on a regular basis, try not to be controlled by commitments in relation to your daily obligations and responsibilities including work, study and family. Rather than change your obligations and responsibilities, work your practice around them, including using the responsibilities and obligations themselves as opportunities to practise mindfulness.

As well as the effects of mindfulness practice, these approaches themselves can also be brought into a variety of life situations beyond practice, including with goal-setting. Though it helps to have a goal as a motivating factor, rather than seeing a goal or aspiration as a perceived future, it may help to see it as a motivational factor to undertake a practice or a challenge. Applying mindfulness en route can help you to be with each moment towards your goal, rather than being lost in the goal or aspiration itself.

BIBLIOGRAPHY

Ajahn Chah (2007) *Everything is Teaching Us.* Hemel Hempstead: Amaravati Publications. Available at www.amaravati.org/teachings/index, accessed on 17 August 2013.

Csikszentmihalyi, M. (1998) *Finding Flow – The Psychology of Engagement with Everyday Life.* New York: Basic Books.

Kabat-Zinn, J. (2004) *Wherever You Go, There You Are.* London: Piatkus.

Orsillo, S.M. and Roemer, L. (2011) *The Mindful Way Through Anxiety.* New York: Guilford.

Tolle, E. (2005) *The Power of Now – A Guide to Spiritual Enlightenment.* London: Hodder and Stoughton.

Williams, M. and Penman, D. (2011) *Mindfulness – The Eight-Week Meditation Programme for a Frantic World.* London: Piatkus.

USEFUL RESOURCES

Autism Spectrum Counselling and Training (ASPECT)

www.aspectcounsel.co.uk

Provides specialist counselling and therapy, including mindfulness-based therapies, to people on the autistic spectrum and their families.

Be Mindful, Mindfulness Training Australia

www.bemindful.com.au

Provides mindfulness courses for the general public, in schools, healthcare and commercial settings.

Center for Mindfulness in Medicine, Healthcare, and Society, University of Massachusetts Medical School

www.umassmed.edu/cfm

Founded by Jon Kabat-Zinn, the centre developed the eight-week MSBR programme and also conducts research into mindfulness.

Centre for Mindfulness Research and Practice, Bangor University

www.bangor.ac.uk/mindfulness

Provides training to professionals in mindfulness-based approaches and offers classes in mindfulness-based stress reduction (MBSR) and mindfulness-based cognitive therapy (MBCT).

Centre for Mindfulness Studies, Toronto

www.mindfulnessstudies.com

Offers mindfulness-based therapies for the general public and professional training for healthcare professionals.

Institute for Mindfulness-based Approaches (IMA)

www.institute-for-mindfulness.eu

Based in Germany, IMA provides training in mindfulness approaches to education and healthcare providers throughout Europe.

Mindfulness Amstelveen

www.mindfulness-amstelveen.nl

Provides eight-week mindfulness training courses in Dutch and English.

Mindfulness Denmark

www.mindfulness-denmark.dk

Provides courses, retreats and training on mindfulness, including the eight-week MBSR course.

Mindfulness in Life

www.mindfulnessinlife.co.uk

Provides MBSR and MBCT courses to the general public.

Mindfulness in Schools Project

www.mindfulnessinschools.org

Researches, encourages and supports teaching of secular mindfulness in schools.

Mindfulness Training New Zealand

www.mindfulness-training.co.nz

Offers mindfulness-based initiatives/courses in healthcare, commercial settings and public retreats.

Oxford Mindfulness Centre

www.oxfordmindfulness.org

Offers mindfulness training to professionals and patients, including clinical services, and also conducts extensive research in the field.

INDEX